NEXT-GEN TEACHING
AI STRATEGIES FOR MODERN EDUCATORS

Chris LaFata, Ed.D.

For the front-line teachers and instructors
giving their all every day.

ALSO BY CHRIS LAFATA

Fiction

Washington's Providence

Table of Contents

INTRODUCTION

WELCOME TO THE WILD WEST

FOR any generation born before 1980, the encyclopedia was probably a first source for any kind of research assignment. We were limited to the books, magazines, and newspapers we had on hand. I had a set of junior encyclopedias someone had given to my family. Each volume was about a quarter-inch thick. It served my needs because teachers knew students didn't have the resources to do in-depth research outside of the school or local library.

My strongest memory of seventh grade was when my English teacher tasked me with finding out the name the Secretary of the Interior. I had never even heard of the Secretary of the Interior. I didn't want to let the teacher down, and if I'm being honest, I was afraid to not know the answer the next time we had class. I went home and cracked open my handy junior encyclopedia even though I knew the current Secretary of the Interior wouldn't be listed. Maybe the job description would be outlined or at least a list of former secretaries. No such luck. I asked my parents. They hadn't heard of the job title either.

During the next class, the teacher didn't ask me about it. He forgot. I was saved! I tried the school library just in case it came up in class the next day. I couldn't find the answer there either. I can't remember if I asked the librarian for help. I probably didn't.

The next week, the teacher called on me and asked if I had found the name of the Secretary of the Interior. He hadn't forgotten. He had given me a week to locate the answer because he knew my resources were limited. I had nothing. I was ashamed. It was one of the first times in my life when I wasn't a "model student."

Nowadays, we don't need to look up questions like this. There's no encyclopedia to crack open or library to visit. We don't even have to touch a computer keyboard. All we have to do is ask Siri or Alexa, "Who is the Secretary of the Interior?" The answer: Deb Harland. It takes 4 seconds to get the information. We can even ask, "Who was the Secretary of the Interior in 1986?" The answer: Donald Hodel. That took another 4 seconds. Artificial Intelligence (AI) made that Herculean task for a mid-80s seventh grader ridiculously easy.

Until recently, AI has felt like more of a fictional device than anything we would encounter in our day-to-day lives. Those of us who grew up in the 80s and 90s feared Skynet "becoming aware" and unleashing the Terminator on us. Or maybe you're more partial to the lovable WALL-E who just wants to find love and make the world a cleaner place.

Doesn't it feel like—seemingly out of nowhere—stories involving AI are everywhere? Our newsfeeds are filled with articles about AI. A quick Google search in mid-May, 2024 revealed titles like, *How is Generative AI Changing Education?* (Manning, 2024), *UM Teaching Graduate Jumps Aboard AI Education Train* (Kuntz, 2024), and *AI is Changing How Schools Teach. They Need Guidance To Do It Wisely* (Cagle, 2024). In my role as an academic dean at a small two-year college, I get dozens of emails and solicitations regarding AI a week (I'm writing this on a Tuesday afternoon. I've had six AI solicitations today). All of this happened in less than two years.

From the moment OpenAI launched ChatGPT in November of 2022, the world changed.

Is that too dramatic?

Maybe, but I believe it will be viewed as one of those moments where life as we know it would never be the same. Can you imagine living without a smartphone? Or the internet? Or the microprocessor? Or Star Wars? This isn't some fad that's going to go away. The genie is out of the bottle. In Andrew Ng's (2023) TED Talk, *AI Isn't the Problem - It's the Solution,* he famously said, "AI is the new electricity."

With every new technology, there's fear that some jobs will become obsolete—and it's absolutely true. The Luddites famously destroyed the mechanized textile looms that threatened their livelihoods. As cities moved to electric street lighting, lamplighters were out of a job. The automobile put a cramp in horse buggy production. Technology has eliminated the need for bowling pinsetters, switchboard operators, newspaper typesetters, and countless factory line workers. Part of the alarm this time around is AI has the ability to replace white-color jobs. When I was a full-time instructor, I got emails asking if I wanted a textbook publisher's software to grade papers for me. I thought, "No way. I don't want to be replaced by a computer." Well, the technology is here now, and part of the initial panic involves the fear of being rendered obsolete.

But it's not all doom and gloom. I taught economics for over twenty years and the pattern has always been: some jobs disappear, new jobs are created. Growing up, I never knew there'd be content creators, social media managers, online instructors, Uber drivers, or even website developers. I'm still not sure what a content creator actually does that's productive, but it's a profession.

AI is going to do the same thing. Some jobs will become obsolete while others that we haven't even thought of yet will be created. Isn't it our role as educators to prepare the next generation to adapt and be productive in the modern economy? Harvard Business School Professor Karim Lakhani (2023) said, "AI is not going to replace humans, but humans with AI are going to replace humans without AI." He's on to something. To anyone thinking teachers will be replaced by AI, they won't. But the way they teach will change—or perhaps they *will be replaced* by teachers who use AI.

Education has seen disruptors before. I remember doing long division with a pencil and paper and the teacher saying it was important to learn because we wouldn't always have a calculator handy. Now, we all have smartphones with us almost every minute of the day, and they all have calculator apps. In fact, we don't even need to plug in the equations. We simply pick up our phones and ask Siri or Alexa (both examples of AI) our question and instantly receive the answer. Students no longer sit in libraries to look up information from books in the collection. They visit libraries for quiet places to study and to access information from web sites and online databases.

We've been interacting with AI for a long time. Remember the paperclip, Clippy, that would show up in Microsoft Office? For those of you who weren't using Word and Excel in the late 1900s, Clippy (short for Clippit) was a virtual assistant (Cain, 2017). If you started typing a letter in Word, Clippy would appear with a word bubble that said something like, "Hey, it looks like you're writing a letter," and offer to format it for you. Eventually, Clippy became annoying because it couldn't tell the difference between your first letter and your twentieth letter. It treated every instance as a first occurrence. Users looked for ways to turn off the assistant and Microsoft eventually discontinued Clippy. If you're feeling nostalgic, there are Clippy desktop apps you can download that resurrect the icon—you know—in case you have forgotten how to format a letter.

Our interactions with AI haven't all been as obvious as Clippy. Google has been the largest AI influence in our lives up until this point. Many people think Google is a search engine company. That would be incorrect. It's an AI company. This is the reason my Google search would look different from your Google search. The results differ based on search history, zip codes, personal preferences, and whatever else goes into the algorithm. Google is anticipating the results it thinks you want. A similar process determines the sponsored ads you see at the top of your search.

The process of anticipating our needs happens again and again whether we're scrolling through videos on YouTube or Tik Tok or looking for something to watch on Netflix. I've discovered new music based on Spotify and Apple Music suggestions, and I can't tell you the number of times Amazon suggested a product to me where I thought, "Hey, I really *do* want that!"

As you think about AI, think in terms of the program trying to anticipate what you need. When you're typing an email on your phone or computer, the autocomplete is trying to anticipate the word or phrase before you finish the keystrokes. That's basically what ChatGPT is: autocomplete on steroids (Ré, 2023). Instead of completing a word or phrase, it anticipates paragraphs or entire articles or books based on a few instructions from the user. The more you interact with AI, the better it will anticipate the types of tasks you want to complete, and it will write it in the style that best suits your needs.

If you're reading this, you either want to know what all the fuss is about or you want to know how to manage and adapt your instructional methods. This is not a comprehensive history of AI nor is it a exhaustive list or summary of all the different AI options available to teachers. This isn't an entirely academic work (I want people to read it) or a fluff piece (I've included references. They're just not from academic journals). Let's call it a hybrid.

The point of this book is to provide easy-to-follow, understandable strategies for making your life easier so you can focus on more important things, like teaching. In the following chapters, we'll take a look at AI in the modern classroom, personalizing feedback for our students, creating lesson plans in seconds, writing effective prompts, simplifying confusing concepts, customizing learning pathways, empowering how to teach students to use AI for good and not evil, ethical concerns, and what the future might bring.

As you go through the concepts and complete the exercises, keep in mind there's no perfect way to do any of this. Remember, the AI is learning just like you are. A prompt that you type will generate a different response than a prompt that I type. It's trying to anticipate *your* desires, not anyone else's. We're entering uncharted territory. It's the Wild West out there. Let's get started.

CHAPTER 1

NAVIGATING AI IN THE MODERN CLASSROOM

A teacher quite savvy and wise
Embraced AI with bright, eager eyes
With lessons enhanced,
And learning advanced
The class soared to new heights and highs
—ChatGPT

NOW that you know a little about what AI is, let's explore a little deeper. While discussing AI within the context of this book, we're referring to something called a Large Language Model (LLM). ChatGPT is an LLM. Claude is an LLM. So is Google Gemini (formerly Bard). LLMs can generate text, answer questions, and perform creative tasks such as the limerick at the beginning of the chapter. It's like having a conversation with the internet. If you do a Google search, sometimes you get the results you want. Sometimes you don't. If you don't, you start the search over. LLMs work different. If you don't get what you're looking for, you ask follow-up questions. As the LLM learns what you're after, it tries to anticipate your needs. This is where the "autocomplete on steroids" comes from (Ré, 2023).

So how does this work? The easiest way is to explain what the "GPT" in ChatGPT means. It stands for Generative Pre-trained Transformer. Got it? No? I have a background in teaching economics and always joked that economists were terrible at naming things. It seems tech guys are terrible too, but in this case, GPT makes sense. Let's break it down.

Generative means that we're asking the programming to "generate" the next word, phrase, idea, or limerick.

Pre-trained means once we've taught the programming the simple task, it can repeat that task.

Transformer is the statistical model that tries to guess the word, phrase, idea, or limerick and make an informed prediction.

Let's say I asked you to fill in the blank for the following, how would you answer?

Three blind _____.

To be or not to _____.

Roses are red, violets are _____.

Four score and seven _____.

You probably did this without even thinking: mice, be, blue, years ago. You've been *pre-trained* from hearing this over and over. If I asked you to be creative with your answers, you could come up with a number of answers, and you could do it easily because you've had years of experience.

Computers don't have this luxury. Programmers had to feed millions (trillions, actually) of words to have a dataset large enough to sound natural to humans. It took 45 terabytes of data, or about 12 trillion words, to train ChatGPT-3 (Bowen & Watson, 2024). For those non-tech nerds who don't know what a terabyte is, a byte is 1 character, like the letter "L" on a keyboard. If the average English word averages 5 characters, that would be 5 bytes per word. One terabyte is 1 trillion characters, or 200 billion words. If you're a math nerd instead of a tech nerd, you're probably thinking: 12 trillion words at 5 bytes per word actually equals 60 terabytes. In reality, the data were filtered before running the models to train ChatGPT-3 anyway, so the dataset would have been considerably less than 45 terabytes. In case you're wondering where the data came from, it was about eight years' worth of web crawling, text from Reddit, full text from books, and Wikipedia (Cooper, 2023).

People are terrible at comprehending large numbers. Let's try to put this into perspective. If you had a book with 300 words per page, 12 trillion words would make the book about 40 billion pages long (about 333,333,333 War and Peaces). According to

Wikipedia (and we all know how much teachers love Wikipedia), there are 6,824,094 articles containing over 4.5 billion words (Wikimedia, 2024). That means 2,666.67 Wikipedias could fit into the dataset used to train ChatGPT-3. You don't need to remember all this. Just know it was A LOT OF WORDS, and that LLMs have been trained on more words than any person could possibly read in a thousand lifetimes.

LLMs comb through the datasets and learn patterns in language. When you type a prompt into ChatGPT, you're getting the most statistically likely response for that prompt. Since we already learned that AI is trying to find the response that *you* are looking for based on your own queries, search history, context, etc., you will likely get different responses when entering prompts but probably get into the ballpark.

For example, if you're trying to find out what professions someone with a psychology degree can pursue, the LLM will try to make an informed prediction. Here are the results from ChatGPT-3.5:

1. Clinical Psychologist
2. Counseling Psychologist
3. School Psychologist
4. Industrial-Organizational Psychologist
5. Forensic Psychologist
6. Health Psychologist
7. Sports Psychologist
8. Researcher/Academic
9. Human Resources Specialist
10. Social Worker

This doesn't mean psychology majors are limited to only ten professions. It doesn't even mean these are the top ten professions. It means that based on the dataset that trained the LLM (in this case, ChatGPT-3.5), these are ten *likely* responses. Now that you have a better idea about how LLMs work, let's step into the classroom.

The Rise of AI in the Classroom

As educators, we've had access to AI tools for a while. As we got away from traditional paper textbooks and incorporated more ebooks, textbook publishers added tools to help students master material. Additionally, tech companies started developing tools for students to boost productivity. Among these tools were Adaptive Learning Platforms, Intelligent Tutoring Systems, and Automated Grading Systems.

Adaptive learning platforms are computer-based assignments that ask students questions. If the question is answered incorrectly, an explanation of why the question is wrong is presented along with a new, similar question. If the next question is answered correctly, the student moves to the next concept. If not, another explanation is given along with another new, similar question and so on.

Personally, I like students having to master concepts before proceeding through the material. Khan Academy is a great example of adaptive learning being used for math students. But adaptive learning isn't just for math. There are adaptive learning platforms for foreign languages, such as Duolingo and Babbel. There are also tools for subject areas in Reading and Language Arts, Science, Economics, and General Studies.

Intelligent Tutoring Systems (ITS) are similar to Adaptive Learning systems. They also provide personalized instruction and feedback based on student responses, but they take it a step further by providing personalized, just-in-time instruction and feedback the same way a real-life tutor would. Think of applications like ALEKS or Carnegie Learning's Cognitive Tutor.

Let's say a student is learning how to solve quadratic equations. In an adaptive learning system, the student works through the problems. After each question, the system adapts the content. If the student is struggling, it asks similar questions. Alternatively, if the student demonstrates understanding, it poses more advanced problems with the difficulty adjusted accordingly.

In an ITS, as the student works through each problem, each step of the student's progress is analyzed. Feedback and hints are offered based on the student's approach to the problem.

Automated Grading Systems use AI to grade and assess student assignments and tests. These are excellent tools—especially in large classroom situations. Assessments won't be limited to multiple choice exams because short answer and essay questions can be graded in a matter of seconds. It saves time but also eliminates grading fatigue, where teachers tire after grading multiple papers and become less thorough. I know I've been guilty of this in my career. Another benefit is the elimination of

13

grading bias and the subjective nature of grading essays (Kim & Araujo, 2021). A good example of a company that's worked in this space is Grammarly. Grammarly is an AI-powered assistant that offers feedback on someone's writing. It provides spelling and grammar checks, sentence clarity suggestions, better word choices, a plagiarism checker, and it can even detect the tone. It works across platforms and can be used on computers and mobile devices (Grammarly, 2024). Keep in mind that writing can be nuanced, so there's still a debate as to whether the system can understand subtleties and context that a human grader would catch.

There's also a dark side to AI in the classroom, and it's when students use technology to cheat. Math teachers have dealt with students using AI to do homework for years. Apps like Photomath and Gauth allow users to snap a picture of a math equation and have the computer solve it and provide step-by-step instructions—even if the problem was handwritten. This is fine if students are trying to understand how to solve problems, but not-so-fine if students are using it to cheat.

I know a College Algebra instructor that catches cheaters by adding Calculus 1 questions to exams. Students that can solve those problems perfectly on tests are asked to solve similar problems during office hours in front of the teacher. Needless to say, a few cheating confessions emerged after students couldn't solve the equations without the app.

As students rely more and more on apps like Grammarly to submit "perfect" papers, they run the risk of their work being detected as AI generated. There's a fine line between a tool and a crutch.

The release and proliferation of LLMs allow teachers the flexibility to take aspects of the systems and customize them for their own courses. This will help personalize learning for students on a level never before seen in education and increase engagement. It will also free up time for teachers to do more of what they love to do: teach.

Using AI to Increase Equity

Equity in education suggests all students have an equal chance to succeed, no matter their family's socioeconomic background (Harris & Jones, 2020). The Covid-19 pandemic exposed a lot of inequities in education as classes moved to remote learning, and many students struggled finding access to adequate computers and/or internet access. In many states, funding increased to provide better access. In June of 2023, the Biden Administration unveiled a $42 billion plan to create universal internet access by 2030 (Mason & Renshaw, 2023). We're not 100% where we want to be, but we're headed in the right direction.

Instructors have the ability to create personalized learning paths for all students, no matter the background (more on this in Chapter 6). Students can use AI to get instant feedback on assignments before they are submitted. If used properly, AI can be a great tool to help teach concepts to students and give everyone the support they need no matter their socioeconomic status. Every student can have a personal tutor for any subject who is available 24 hours a day, patient, and free.

The possibilities for this are tremendous. If taught early and used properly, it could make a large dent in the achievement gap. When referring to *achievement gap*, there is no single gap, but many gaps in achievement based on comparing different groups (Downey et al., 2009). Teachers face these gaps when interacting with students from different socioeconomic backgrounds, genders, races, and nationalities. AI can help bridge these gaps by providing customized feedback and giving each individual the help needed to master content.

Standardized test scores have long reflected racial inequities, where White and Asian-American students outperforming Black and Latino students. During the Covid-19 pandemic, many colleges and universities eliminated the testing requirement for admissions, including the Ivy League along with Ivy Plus schools, like Duke, the University of Chicago, and MIT. But in 2024, Dartmouth College became the first Ivy League school to reinstate standardized SAT or ACT scores as part of the application process. This came after a joint study with Brown University determined test scores could predict first-year student success better than other factors such as high school GPA. Additionally, higher test scores enhance schools' ability to identify less-advantaged applicants (Altcheck, 2024).

This begs the question as to whether Black or Latino students are performing worse on standardized tests due to their race or because of the likelihood that these students are coming from lower socioeconomic communities. Given this situation, it's logical because these students may not have had the resources to take the tests multiple times or receive additional tutoring to improve their scores on the SAT or ACT. AI can be a potential solution. To see it in action, try this:

> **Prompt:** Create a 25-question test that could be used to prep for the SAT in English.

You'll find the AI assistant will draft a 25-question practice test. There's no expensive SAT workbook to purchase or tutor to pay. Students will be able to take more control of their learning and use AI to identify their weaknesses and develop strategies to improve their times. In my experience, a good chunk of the battle in scoring well on standardized tests is having a strategy on how to take them rather than knowing all the content.

Navigating the Modern Classroom

The best advice for navigating the modern classroom is to approach it with a growth mindset. This is the idea that abilities can be developed through perseverance and hard work and that we can all grow no matter where we're starting from. As mentioned earlier, the genie is out of the bottle. Fighting it is like trying to catch and hold on to waves at the seashore. Reading this and learning about the new opportunities AI affords is a great start. As Carol Dweck said, when you have a growth mindset, challenges are exciting rather than threatening (Dweck, 2006). Educators must consider this while grappling with the greatest education disruptor since the internet (or Covid-19). If your institution or district offers training, take advantage of it and attend. Remember, things change all the time. Businesses have been formed for the sole purpose of providing training on AI, and these webinars and presentations will each have a handful of nuggets you can take and apply right away.

There are some ethical concerns when interacting or using AI-generated content. Remember, the output you see is the most statistically likely response it thinks you want to see. If you ask it to write a story or generate an image, it's possible it will spit out stereotypes. There is going to be a learning curve for both the AI and the users. We'll cover more about this in Chapter 8 when discussing ethical issues with AI.

Focus on using AI as a tool, not a substitute for doing the work. As you interact with it to generate lesson plans or help grade assignments, don't assume the response you get is the only response or the best response. Every educator wants to teach students to be excellent critical thinkers and we want our graduates to enter the workforce prepared for whatever may come. It's good to have a similar approach when using AI in the classroom.

In the next chapter, we'll jump into personalizing learning experiences for our students. Before we do that, it's important for you to have access to a LLM (reminder, Large Language

Model) so you can follow along or jot down notes to try on your own. In order to access an LLM, you'll need to choose an Application Programming Interface (API). Think of them like middlemen that translate the information you want to the computer server you're connecting to. If you post a status update on Facebook from your computer and another from your phone, APIs translate that information so your friends can see the update. If you order food at a restaurant, the API would be the server taking your order and passing it on to the kitchen (Tray.io, 2019). For the rest of this book, let's just refer to APIs as AI assistants. If you're anything like me, you have enough acronyms in your life already.

Table 1 lists a few popular AI Assistants (at the time of this writing) and their distinguishing features. Choose at least one, or a few if you're feeling inspired. You will be asked to create a login because the AI will attempt to learn your habits and give you exactly what you're looking for when you interact with it. You do not have to enter any credit card or payment information. All the AI assistants listed have free options, even though they might prompt you to upgrade to a paid version.

Table 1: Popular APIs and Their Distinguishing Features

API	LLM	Parent Company	Distinguishing Features
ChatGPT	ChatGPT-3.5 (free) GPT-4 GPT-4o (upgrade)	OpenAI	• Large-scale pre-training on diverse datasets allowing multi-turn conversations • Natural language understanding and generation • Not connected to the Internet. Model trained on data available to September, 2021.
Perplexity	ChatGPT-3.5 (free) GPT-4, GPT-4o (upgrade)	Perplexity	• Works like a search engine that uses ChatGPT to synthesize answers in a conversational way. • Provides citations for every piece of information presented in its answers. • Tries to provide unbiased and diverse information to help eliminate filter bubbles and echo chambers.
Copilot API	ChatGPT-4	Microsoft	• Emphasizes responsible AI principles: transparency, fairness, and ethical considerations in the development and deployment of AI systems. • Designed to be integrated into Microsoft 365 apps (Word, Excel, Powerpoint, Outlook, Teams)
Meta AI	Llama 2	Meta (Facebook)	• Can understand and respond in multiple languages • Conversational AI • Multimodal Interaction - Can process multiple forms of input, such as text, images, and voice commands

API	LLM	Parent Company	Distinguishing Features
Claude	Claude	Anthropic	• Emphasizes safety and ethical behavior with built-in safeguards to avoid harmful or biased content. • Specialized for open-ended dialog that can assist with everything from analysis and writing to coding and math problems. • Multilingual support
Gemini	Gemini	Google	• Prioritizes accurate and unbiased information while limiting bias and misinformation • Can access information from constantly update sources. • Integrates with Google products

Examples in this book will be taken from the free versions of the AI assistants from Table 1, and it's possible by the time you read this, some may no longer exist. Things change. In 2023, Bard was Google's flagship assistant. It's now called Gemini. GPT-4o (the *o* stands for *omni*) was released after the introduction was written for this book. This is by no means a comprehensive list, only a list of the more popular ones at the time of this writing that I thought would be most beneficial to educators.

Khanmigo from Khan Academy offers free AI tools for educators providing everything from discussion prompts to assessments to lesson plans. Until recently it was a paid option. Check it out! It's user-friendly and has a lot of great resources.

Before we jump in, recall that just because you get an AI response from one of the assistants, it doesn't necessarily mean the response is true. Remember, you're getting the most statistically likely response. There have even been cases where ChatGPT made up information it didn't know.

You may have heard the story about two lawyers getting fined for submitting six legal cases to support their arguments that were "created" by ChatGPT (Neumeister, 2023). In another case, a lawyer was accused of citing three non-existent court cases when appealing for the supervised early release of Michael Cohen, former attorney for Donald Trump (Palmer, 2023). The lesson in both cases is one of caution. LLMs have been known to fabricate (the new term being thrown around is *hallucinate*) information they don't know. This will improve as more users add data and the LLMs learn from interactions with people.

Fortunately, some of the AI assistants offer a workaround. If you create a ChatGPT account, there's an option in settings to Customize ChatGPT. You can create custom instructions and offer information about yourself to help you provide better responses. It will offer suggestions on how to begin, such as adding your location or the kind of work you do. Here are the custom instructions I added for my account:

> *I am a higher education administrator, but I teach college-level classes.*
> *I teach economics and am interested in how people respond to incentives.*
> *I like to write in a clear, concise manner.*

In the next section, you are asked, "How would you like ChatGPT to respond?" This is the area where you can specify how formal you want your responses or the length of the typical response unless otherwise directed. For the second paragraph, I was guided by verbiage suggested in the AI newsletter, aitoolreport.com. Here's mine:

Responses should be relatively short, between 100 and 200 words unless I ask for more.
ChatGPT should remain neutral and not have opinions on topics unless prompted.

You are expected to communicate in a scholarly manner. All statements, beliefs, or data you present must be attributed to a credible and published source. Never fabricate any references. If uncertain about a reference, admit your lack of knowledge. There's no need to mention that you're an AI, as I'm already aware. Reiteration is unnecessary and inefficient. Ensure your replies are concise yet accurate. Use only the essential words without sacrificing the clarity and accuracy of your response. Adhere diligently to my directives. For instance, if I specify a two-sentence reply, provide only two sentences.

Notice that I provided specific instructions on how I want my responses. There's a directive to never make up information it doesn't know. I gave specifications on the length and clarity of responses. I would recommend you set up similar guidelines when you create your account. If you already use ChatGPT, you may already have parameters in place.

ChatGPT isn't the only AI assistant that offers the option to add custom instructions. Perplexity allows you to add personalized information. I pasted my ChatGPT parameters there. It also asks your preferred language and physical location. I couldn't locate an area in the other AI assistants to add these settings, so you'll have to add specific instructions to your prompts (more on this in Chapter 4). I did, however, find a cool setting in Claude with the option to use a dyslexic-friendly font.

Now that you know a little more about LLMs and how we've already had AI in the classroom, let's move on to strategies that will help save time and provide more enriched learning experiences for our students.

Chapter Takeaways

1. Introduction to Artificial Intelligence (AI) and Large Language Models (LLMs).
2. LLMs predict the next word, phrase, or idea based on large datasets and respond to prompts by generating statistically likely answers.
3. Educators have been using AI tools for years in the form of Adaptive Learning Platforms, Intelligent Tutoring Systems, and Automated Grading Systems.
4. AI can help bridge educational inequities by offering personalized learning experiences and providing instant feedback.
5. Educators are advised to approach AI with a growth mindset and remain critical of AI-generated content, being aware of potential biases, inaccuracies, or fabrications.

CHAPTER 2

AMPLIFIED PERSONAL FEEDBACK

Feedback is really a necessary part of any complex learning.
There's no instruction so flawless that people are going
to learn something perfectly without feedback.
— Cathy Chase

WHEN I first taught adjunct courses in the early 2000s, there was an emphasis placed on instructors providing detailed, custom feedback. That was fine if I was teaching one class with 20-30 students, but not when I taught 6 or 7 classes and had 150-200 students. Grading fatigue became a real thing—especially when grading the same essay over and over (and over and over…). I worked through this by creating a spreadsheet with a list of detailed comments that I wrote and organized them by the typical response. If you teach a course long enough, you get a feel for how students will answer certain prompts. I ended up with a very basic *If…then* system.

In those days, we had to download the Word documents, save them to a local drive, insert our comments, and re-upload for the students to view the feedback. If a student wrote an "A" paper by making a compelling argument using credible sources with no spelling and grammar errors, I would copy and paste a detailed comment from my spreadsheet and use the insert comment feature in Word. If the student's essay didn't use a credible source or had spelling or grammar issues, I would paste a comment indicating the issues and highlight specific examples in the paper. The process was tedious.

I continued a similar process for many years. Even though most of us no longer have to download student papers, the process for adding feedback hasn't changed. I still used a list of frequently used comments to help make grading more efficient. Even with the timesavers in place, grading fatigue would still crop up after reading multiple essays on the same topic.

The more I progressed through my education, the more I looked forward to hearing what the instructor had to say about my work (this was directly correlated with me becoming a more engaged learner). I wasn't as focused on the grade. I approached school with the idea that if I gave my best effort, the grades would take care of themselves. It was disappointing to get back an "A" paper (not disappointing) with feedback that said, "Great job" (disappointing). It's the equivalent of sending a long text message to someone and getting a thumbs up response. Put forth some effort people.

AI allows us to give specific, tailored feedback to each student response or assignment and address specific strengths, weaknesses, and areas for improvement—and do it in seconds. We can even create (or have the AI create) grading rubrics with assigned point values that grade papers.

Here's a specific example I used in my macroeconomics courses. When we got to the chapter on productivity, I always brought up Thomas Robert Malthus. For those of you who did not take my macroeconomics class, Malthus was an eighteenth-century scholar who said the human population was growing at a faster rate than could be fed, and that civilization was basically destined for poverty and an overall miserable experience. Here are the exact instructions for the assignment:

> Robert Malthus argued that an ever-increasing population would continually strain society's ability to provide for itself and mankind was doomed forever to live in poverty. Since his prediction in 1798, the world population has increased sixfold. Worldwide living standards have increased and malnutrition is less common. Why was Malthus wrong?
> * (1-2 pages, double-spaced)
> * Use at least 1 outside source to support your answer.
> * No Wikipedia or Investopedia

I would grade about 100 of these during that assignment week. My course was set up where assignments were always due Sunday at 11:59pm. My goal was to have assignments graded by Wednesday (not always successfully) to give students time to view their feedback and understand where they could improve for future assignments. That meant I had 3 days to grade 100 assignments. I used a grading rubric that assigned points for answering the question completely, utilizing an organized and well-thought argument, applying appropriate critical thinking with multiple viewpoints, and using correct spelling and grammar. I would typically highlight specific problem areas and offer quick comments. I would almost never summarize the student's specific paper. I would add a final summary similar to this:

> Yes, Malthus failed to account for advancements in technology, production growth, trade, travel, etc... We give him a hard time, but he was using the information available to him. Remember, he wrote at the beginning of the Industrial Revolution. He had no way to anticipate the changes that would come. Predictions are based on a snapshot of where we're at in a particular moment. As the variables change—and they ALWAYS do—the outcomes will

change. Think about all the resources that have been saved since the advent of the smart phone. We no longer need alarm clocks, GPS devices in our cars, home telephones, large desktop computers (for some), pagers, etc... Innovations like that change the variables for a question about resources.

That would be the extent of the feedback. Not great. I was able to impart what I wanted the student to remember, but aside from a few minor comments, the feedback was very cookie-cutter. I thought I was doing a good job because students told me so in end-of-course surveys by saying they appreciated the feedback. It makes me wonder what kind of feedback they received in their other classes (probably something along the lines of *great job*). Shute (2008) said feedback should be specific and clear, timely, and actionable. Sadly, my feedback was none of these.

After ChatGPT was released, I recognized the potential impact to education and jumped headfirst into familiarizing myself with it. I learned we could upload student assignments to ChatGPT and ask it to provide feedback. It could give quick, specific feedback and offer areas of improvement for not only spelling and grammar but more nuanced things like tone. It felt like a game changer. Imagine the time it could save grading essays. It could free up instructors to assign more complex assignments and stay away from multiple choice assessments because the time required to grade would be drastically reduced.

But what about ethical concerns? Is there a violation of student privacy if we upload a paper to one of the LLMs? It will become part of the training model. If a student uploads personal details about themselves or someone else, it could potentially be used in a response for someone else down the road. For this reason, many businesses have policies prohibiting employees from uploading proprietary information. We heard similar concerns when instructors started uploading assignments to plagiarism checkers due to the systems creating permanent archives of the submissions (Brinkman, 2012). Teachers should exercise discretion when uploading student assignments and remove names and identifying characteristics. There is an option in ChatGPT to manually remove your chat history and request that OpenAI (ChatGPT's parent company) delete your past conversations (Ryan, 2023). We'll revisit this topic in Chapter 8.

I decided to see what ChatGPT could do to make my feedback more personal to the student yet keep some of the main points I wanted the student to learn. Going back to the Malthus assignment, I created a series of prompts to train the system to respond how I wanted it to respond. A prompt is a command you give to the AI with specific instructions. We'll cover this in depth in Chapter 4. Here's how I set it up for the Malthus assignment:

> **Prompt 1:** I'm going to give you a writing prompt that I asked students to answer. You don't have to answer it. Next, I'm going to submit student responses one at a time and provide instructions for you. Do you understand?
>
> **ChatGPT:** Yes, I understand. Please provide the prompt when you're ready.
>
> **Prompt 2:** Robert Malthus argued that an ever-increasing population would continually strain society's ability to

provide for itself and mankind was doomed forever to live in poverty. Since his prediction in 1798, the world population has increased sixfold. Worldwide living standards have increased and malnutrition is less common. Why was Malthus wrong?
* (1-2 pages, double-spaced)
* Use at least 1 outside source to support your answer.
* No Wikipedia or Investopedia

ChatGPT: Understood. Please proceed with the submission of the student responses, and let me know if you need any specific instructions for each response.

Prompt 3: For the following responses, write appropriate feedback from a college instructor to a student based on the response to the Malthus question. Did the student answer why Malthus was wrong and use an outside source? Include areas for improvement and summarize in 150 words or less. Do you understand?

ChatGPT: Yes, I understand. Please go ahead and submit the student response for evaluation.

Note that in the first prompt, I told ChatGPT not to answer. This was after some trial and error, where I pasted the essay question to give context, and the AI proceeded to answer it. I also asked the clarifying, *Do you understand* question to make sure we were on the same page. Notice ChatGPT's response after submitting the assignment instructions. It knows what to expect next and asked for the student responses. Finally, in prompt 3, I gave specific instructions on how I wanted the feedback presented. I asked from the perspective of a college instructor to a student. I asked whether the student answered the question (shockingly, some students don't read the instructions thoroughly). I also requested feedback on areas of improvement and asked for a summary in 150 words or less (150 words is probably too much, but this is what I did). Again, I asked for understanding.

Next, I pasted the student's paper. I did not include the student's name or any identifying characteristics. I always asked for APA format, but I never included headers or title pages when submitting the assignment to ChatGPT. Here's the feedback:

> **ChatGPT:** You effectively discussed why Malthus was wrong, highlighting the failure to recognize human adaptability and the detrimental consequences of his proposed solutions. The inclusion of the outside source supports the argument, adding depth to the analysis. However, the response could be improved by providing more specific examples and elaborating on how education and resource provision contribute to addressing population-related challenges. Additionally, while the reference to China's one-child policy is relevant, further analysis of its consequences would strengthen the argument. Furthermore, the response could benefit from clearer organization and transitions between points to enhance coherence. Overall, you demonstrate a solid understanding of the topic and effectively incorporate external evidence, but further development of examples and refinement of structure would enhance the clarity and depth of the response.

Did I get what I asked for? The tone of the feedback seems appropriate for college-level students. The first sentence mentions the student effectively discussed why Malthus was wrong and includes reasons even in the paper. The outside source was mentioned. Areas for improvement were stated along with a nice little summary—and it did it in 126 words.

Next, I sandwiched my instructor feedback around the AI feedback:

Yes, Malthus failed to account for advancements in technology, production growth, trade, travel, etc... We give him a hard time, but he was using the information available to him. Remember, he wrote at the beginning of the Industrial Revolution. He had no way to anticipate the changes that would come. You effectively discussed why Malthus was wrong, highlighting the failure to recognize human adaptability and the detrimental consequences of his proposed solutions. The inclusion of the outside source supports the argument, adding depth to the analysis. However, the response could be improved by providing more specific examples and elaborating on how education and resource provision contribute to addressing population-related challenges. Additionally, while the reference to China's one-child policy is relevant, further analysis of its consequences would strengthen the argument. Furthermore, the response could benefit from clearer organization and transitions between points to enhance coherence. Overall, you demonstrate a solid understanding of the topic and effectively incorporate external evidence, but further development of examples and refinement of structure would enhance the clarity and depth of the response.

Predictions are based on a snapshot of where we're at in a particular moment. As the variables change—and they ALWAYS do—the outcomes will change. Think about all the resources that have been saved since the advent of the smart phone. We no longer need alarm clocks, GPS devices in our cars, home telephones, large desktop computers (for some), pagers, etc... Innovations like that change the variables for a question about resources.

Could I have handled my prompts better? Probably. Any skill gets better the more we practice, but it felt like it was a good start. Knowing what I know now, I could have trained the AI to provide feedback inside my feedback, creating a "feedback sandwich." It's a work in progress. As you start creating your own feedback prompts, you'll probably come up with your own (better) ideas and time-saving strategies.

Although AI can provide specific and tailored feedback, it could still have trouble with more sophisticated and nuanced arguments. It's essential to monitor and refine the feedback provided by AI assistants to ensure accuracy and relevance to student learning.

AI-Created Rubrics

Most teachers and instructors use some sort of grading rubric to assess student work. A rubric makes it easy for students to see where they did well and focus on areas they need to improve. Even teachers who don't use rubrics have something in mind as far as what is "A" work versus "C" work. I would argue that the more experienced you are teaching a specific subject, the quicker you can spot excellent or middling work. The trick is getting your expertise and feedback into the hands of the learner so they can grow. AI can help us do that.

Try this. If you have a rubric, input it into an AI assistant. Create a prompt to have AI generate a gradable rubric based on your criteria. I'll use the one I shared earlier, only this time, we'll have the AI create one in table format and grade a student paper.

Prompt: Create a grading rubric worth 50 total points based on the following criteria: The entire question was answered, 10 points; The response was organized and well-thought out, 10 points; The writing showed an appropriate level of critical thinking and multiple viewpoints were addressed, 20 points; Correct spelling and grammar was used. Sources were cited properly, 10 points. If no sources were listed, the student gets 0 points for that part of the rubric. Create the rubric in table format.

Copilot Response

Table

Criteria	Points
Entire Question Answered	10
Response Organization and Coherence	10
Critical Thinking and Addressing Multiple Viewpoints	20
Correct Spelling, Grammar, and Proper Citations	0 (No sources listed)

Prompt: Next, I'm going to submit the assignment prompt students had to follow. You do not need to answer the question. I want you to understand the expectations for the students. Here's the assignment prompt: Robert Malthus argued that an ever-increasing population would continually strain society's ability to provide for itself and mankind was doomed forever to live in poverty. Since his prediction in 1798, the world population has increased by more than six times. Worldwide living standards have increased and malnutrition is less common. Why was Malthus wrong? What are some more recent predictions you've heard that will doom humanity? Why do you think these predictions will be more or less accurate than Malthus? (1-2 pages, double-spaced) Use at least 1 outside source to support your answer. Do you understand?

Copilot Response: Certainly! I understand the assignment prompt.

Prompt: Here's the student assignment. Grade using the rubric you created and put it in table format. Create a third column for points earned and a fourth column to add specific feedback for the student: *(I pasted the student paper here)*

Copilot Response

Table

Criteria	Points Possible	Points Earned	Feedback
Entire Question Answered	10	10	The submission effectively addresses the Malthusian trap, explaining how agriculture sustains a growing population and the consequences if agriculture doesn't experience growth. Well done!
Response Organization and Coherence	10	10	The submission is well-organized into distinct sections discussing different reasons for Malthus's error. Your clarity in presenting these points is commendable.
Critical Thinking and Addressing Multiple Viewpoints	20	20	You've demonstrated critical thinking by discussing multiple viewpoints related to Malthus's error. The mention of technological advancements, private property rights, and public health adds depth to your analysis. Great job!
Correct Spelling, Grammar, and Proper Citations	10	0	Unfortunately, there are no sources cited in your submission. Remember that proper citations strengthen your arguments and provide evidence. Consider adding relevant sources in future assignments.

I tried the exact same prompts with Google Gemini. Here are the responses:

Gemini Response:

Grading Rubric (Total Points: 50)

Criteria	Description	Points Possible
Comprehensiveness (10 points)	The entire question is answered thoroughly. All key points are addressed.	0 (Not Answered) - 10 (Fully Answered)
Organization & Clarity (10 points)	The response is well-organized and easy to follow. Information flows logically.	0 (Unorganized) - 10 (Clear & Organized)
Critical Thinking & Viewpoints (20 points)	The response demonstrates critical thinking skills. Multiple viewpoints are considered and analyzed.	0 (No Critical Thinking) - 20 (Strong Critical Thinking)
Citations & Grammar (10 points)	Sources are properly cited according to a specified style guide (e.g., MLA, APA). Correct spelling and grammar are used throughout.	0 (No Sources or Errors) - 10 (Sources Cited & Proper Grammar)

⊞ Export to Sheets

Gemini Response:

Grading Rubric (Total Points: 50)

Criteria	Description	Points Possible	Points Earned	Feedback
Comprehensiveness (10 points)	The entire question is answered thoroughly. All key points are addressed.	0 (Not Answered) - 10 (Fully Answered)	7	The essay covers the main ideas but could benefit from a stronger introduction that defines the Malthusian trap and a clearer connection between population control methods and avoiding famine.
Organization & Clarity (10 points)	The response is well-organized and easy to follow. Information flows logically.	0 (Unorganized) - 10 (Clear & Organized)	7	The essay is mostly organized with clear transitions between ideas. However, some improvement could be made by restructuring the introduction and conclusion.

Critical Thinking & Viewpoints (20 points)	The response demonstrates critical thinking skills. Multiple viewpoints are considered and analyzed.	0 (No Critical Thinking) - 20 (Strong Critical Thinking)	12	The essay identifies limitations of Malthus's theory and explores the role of technology and social changes. It would be even stronger by acknowledging potential downsides of some solutions (e.g., environmental impact of some technologies)
Citations & Grammar (10 points)	Sources are properly cited according to a specified style guide (e.g., MLA, APA). Correct spelling and grammar are used throughout.	0 (No Sources or Errors) - 10 (Sources Cited & Proper Grammar)	0	No outside sources are cited. There are some grammatical errors (e.g., missing comma after "nations").

⊞ Export to Sheets

Overall Score: 26/50

Well, look who's the tougher grader. Copilot scored the essay 40/50 while Gemini gave it 26 out of 50 points. The same essay was either an 80% or 52%. Students would be quick to drop instructors that graded that much tougher. In all fairness, Copilot has had much more experience with my interactions and possibly understood I wasn't as tough on students at that level.

If you're wondering, I graded the essay 40/50. The lesson here is to experiment with what works for you and your students.

This works for all grade levels, and you can specify how you want the rubric structured. Here's an example (and preview for the next chapter about having AI help with lesson plans) for a sixth-grade Language Arts class.

> **Prompt:** Create a writing assignment appropriate for a 6th-grade Language Arts class that has them write a story about a person their age growing up in the dust bowl. Create a grading rubric with 5 criteria in table format for the assignment worth 100 points. In the rubric, place an emphasis on sentence structure and grammar more than on the plot of the story.

Copilot Response:
Writing Assignment: "Life in the Dust Bowl"
Task:
Imagine you are a 12-year-old living in the midst of the Dust Bowl during the 1930s. Write a short story about your experiences growing up in this challenging environment. Your story should capture the hardships, resilience, and hope of those who faced dust storms, crop failures, and economic struggles.

Requirements:
Setting and Atmosphere (20 points):
o Create a vivid description of the Dust Bowl setting: the dry, cracked earth, swirling dust storms, and the impact on daily life.
o Use sensory details (sight, sound, smell) to immerse the reader in the time and place.
Character Development (20 points):
o Introduce your main character, a 12-year-old facing adversity.
o Describe their feelings, thoughts, and struggles as they navigate life during the Dust Bowl.

Sentence Structure and Grammar (30 points):
- o Use a variety of sentence types (simple, compound, complex) to enhance your storytelling.
- o Pay attention to subject-verb agreement, verb tenses, and punctuation.
- o Avoid run-on sentences and fragments.

Dialogue (15 points):
- o Include at least one dialogue exchange between characters.
- o Use quotation marks correctly and add dialogue tags (e.g., "Mom," he whispered).

Conclusion and Hope (15 points):
- o Conclude your story with a sense of hope or resilience.
- o Show how your character finds strength despite the challenges.

Grading Rubric:

Table

Criteria	Points Possible	Points Earned	Feedback
Setting and Atmosphere	20		
Character Development	20		
Sentence Structure and Grammar	30		
Dialogue	15		
Conclusion and Hope	15		

As you can see, the AI gives us a great starting point for whatever we're working on. As teachers, we are the experts in the area and know better than anyone what our class needs, so feel free to choose your own grading criteria or assign point totals on your own. You are in control here. Treat the AI like a digital personal assistant.

When we get to Chapter 7, we'll revisit these ideas and offer suggestions for grading expectations and take rubrics to a higher level.

Chapter Takeaways

1. Good feedback is crucial for learning and should be specific and clear, timely, and actionable.
2. AI can provide quick, specific, and personalized feedback and help reduce grading fatigue.
3. AI can also help create detailed grading rubrics with specific feedback.

CHAPTER 3

AI-INFUSED LESSON PLANS

> Technology alone is not enough. It's technology married
> with the liberal arts, married with the humanities,
> that yields us the results that make our hearts sing.
> — Steve Jobs

REMEMBER the first class you taught? The first lesson plan you wrote? How did you go about creating one? Maybe you had a mentor, or you went online and found resources or pre-made lesson plans.

My first experience with lesson planning was during student teaching in the late 1900s. I taught world history to tenth graders at a high school near where I grew up. The lesson had something to do with Russian history. I don't even remember what it was.

All I can recall is the stress of coming up with something that would engage the students and not be too boring.

Many teachers look to their experiences as a student and try to replicate that. In higher education, it might be (or is likely) the traditional lecture format where the instructor pontificates in the front of the room and students take notes from their seats. We all know how awful that is as a student, and no teacher likes to bomb from being too lackluster. So, teachers adapt. They take what works and reuse it for future classes and try new strategies for things that didn't work—or at least that's what I hope they are doing. Effective learning environments are spaces that address the students' needs, interests, and strengths (Johnson, 2023). This is why teachers constantly look for ways to improve engagement through hands-on activities that are collaborative, interactive, and create experiences that help students learn.

Serdyukov and Ryan argue that an effective lesson plan has five components: lesson description, goals and objectives, materials and tools, procedures, and a reflective assessment and evaluation (2008a). We want plans that have clear objectives that are easy to follow.

AI can be a great starting point for generating ideas and can even create content for effective classroom plans. Here's one I like to call the "Mad Libs" approach. If you've been out of elementary school for a while, Mad Libs are games where a person or group is asked to come up with nouns, verbs, adjectives, colors, animals, a famous actor, etc., for a story with key words removed. The second person writes these words into the story. Usually, the words make the story nonsensical and hilarious because, really, who doesn't enjoy, "I was transported to the year 11 where I met a stoic pop tart?" You can create your own stoic pop tarts at madlibs.com or aiadlibs.com.

The idea behind the Mad Libs approach is to create lesson plans that work for any subject or grade level in seconds. Head over to your favorite AI assistant and enter this prompt:

> **Prompt:** Write a lesson plan for a(n) (grade) (subject) class about the (lesson title). Please make it a (type of lesson plan) lesson plan and include an interactive activity for students to apply their learning. You create all the content. It should last about (length of time) minutes.

There are a couple of key parts of this prompt that give the AI enough information to generate what you need. The first is "lesson plan." It's going to come out in a usable format that you can alter as you see fit. The next is grade level. We want our lesson plan to be appropriate for our audience. "Subject" and "Lesson title" are letting us get specific about what we're looking for. If we're discussing the Civil Rights Movement in class, there are many different ways we can go. Civil Rights by itself might be too broad. Be as specific as possible and then expand as needed. We're also including an interactive activity. We want the students to be engaged as much as possible. No more lectures outside of introducing the lesson! We're also having the AI create all the content and fill in the details. Remember, the teacher is the expert here, so if there's a point that is missed in the lesson, you can add it yourself or prompt the AI to add it for you. There's also a command as to the type of lesson plan: Basic, Concept, Skills, Writing, Scaffolded Reading Experience, and Discovery (Johnson, 2017). Finally, we're adding the appropriate length of time for our class, so we don't cram too much or add too little into our plan.

Here's an example (Underlining added for emphasis):

Prompt: Write a lesson plan for an 8th grade science class about the Organization of the Periodic Table. Please make it a basic lesson plan and include an interactive activity for students to apply their learning. You create all the content. It should last about 45 minutes.

Copilot Response:

 Copilot

Certainly! Let's create a basic lesson plan for an 8th-grade science class on the **Organization of the Periodic Table**. This lesson will help students understand how elements are arranged in the periodic table and explore their properties. We'll also include an interactive activity to reinforce their learning.

Periodic Table of the Elements

Lesson Plan: Organization of the Periodic Table

Objective:

- Students will understand the organization of the periodic table, including groups, periods, and trends.

- Students will be able to identify elements based on their atomic number, symbol, and properties.

Duration:

Approximately 45 minutes

Materials Needed:

- Whiteboard or projector for visual aids

- Printed periodic table (one per student or group)

- Colored markers or highlighters

Introduction (10 minutes):

1. **Hook** Begin by asking students if they know what the periodic table is and why it's important. Discuss briefly.

2. Explain that the periodic table is a systematic arrangement of chemical elements based on their atomic properties.

3. Show a large periodic table on the whiteboard or projector.

Main Content (25 minutes):

1. Structure of the Periodic Table (10 minutes):

- Discuss the following points:

    - **Periods**: Rows in the periodic table represent periods. Each period corresponds to a different energy level (shell) in an atom.

    - **Groups/Families**: Columns in the periodic table represent groups or families. Elements within the same group have similar properties.

    - **Atomic Number**: Explain that the atomic number (Z) determines an element's position in the periodic table.

    - **Reading the Table**: Show students how to read the atomic symbol, atomic number, and element name for a few elements.

2. Trends in the Periodic Table (15 minutes):

- Discuss the following trends:

    - **Atomic Radius**: How the size of atoms changes across a period and down a group.

    - **Ionization Energy**: The energy required to remove an electron from an atom.

    - **Electronegativity**: An atom's ability to attract electrons.

    - **Metallic vs. Nonmetallic Properties**: Compare metals and nonmetals.

Interactive Activity (10 minutes):

"Element Scavenger Hunt":

1. Divide students into small groups.

2. Provide each group with a printed periodic table.

3. Give them a list of specific elements (e.g., "Find an alkali metal," "Locate a noble gas," etc.).

4. Students must find the elements on the periodic table and mark them with colored markers or highlighters.

5. Discuss their findings as a class.

Conclusion (5 minutes):

- Recap the key points about the periodic table.

- Ask students to share one interesting fact they learned during the lesson.

Assessment:

- Collect students' completed scavenger hunt sheets to assess their understanding of the periodic table.

Feel free to adapt or modify this lesson plan to suit your classroom needs! If you'd like additional resources, you can explore the American Chemical Society's educational materials related to the periodic table ⁷ . Happy teaching! ✏

I don't remember a lot about the periodic table, but this looks like a good start. It seems age-appropriate (I got the lesson plan idea by asking my eighth-grade daughter what she was studying in science). There's an interactive group activity, and it looks like it can be covered in the time allotted. Notice the graphic of the periodic table in the upper-right side of the screen shot. One of the things I like about Copilot is it provides links to images and videos to some of the prompts. This can be helpful if you're dealing with a difficult concept and need something explained differently. We'll cover more on this in Chapter 5.

Here's another example based on my Malthus lesson from the last chapter:

> **Prompt:** Write a lesson plan for a college economics class about Thomas Robert Malthus. Please make it a basic lesson plan and include an interactive activity for students to apply their learning. You create all the content. It should last about an hour and 15 minutes.
>
> **ChatGPT-3.5 Response:**
>
> **Lesson Plan:** Thomas Robert Malthus and His Economic Theories
>
> **Objective:**
> Students will understand the key contributions of Thomas Robert Malthus to economics, particularly his theories on population growth and resource limitations. They will apply Malthusian principles to modern economic issues through interactive activities.
>
> **Duration:**
> 1 hour and 15 minutes
>
> **Materials:**
> - Whiteboard and markers
> - Projector and computer
> - PowerPoint presentation
> - Handouts with key excerpts from Malthus' "An Essay on the Principle of Population"

- Chart paper and markers for group work

Lesson Structure:
1. Introduction (10 minutes)
- **Instructor Introduction:** Briefly introduce Thomas Robert Malthus and his historical context.
- **Objective Overview:** Explain the goals of the lesson and what students will learn.

2. Lecture: Malthusian Theory (20 minutes)
Presentation Slides:
- Slide 1: Background of Thomas Robert Malthus
- Slide 2: Key concepts from "An Essay on the Principle of Population"
- Slide 3: Malthusian Population Growth Model
- Slide 4: Malthusian Catastrophe
- Slide 5: Criticisms and Modern Relevance

Key Points to Cover:
- Malthus' assertion that population grows geometrically while food supply grows arithmetically.
- The concept of carrying capacity and limits to growth.
- Positive and preventive checks on population (e.g., famine, disease, moral restraint).
- The impact of Malthusian theory on later economic thought and policy.

3. Group Activity: Applying Malthusian Theory (30 minutes)
Divide the Class into Small Groups:
- Assign each group a contemporary issue (e.g., climate change, food security, urbanization).
- Provide handouts with excerpts from Malthus' work and a set of guiding questions.

Activity Instructions:
- Each group discusses how Malthusian theory applies to their assigned issue.
- Groups create a chart or poster summarizing their analysis.
- Include how Malthus' ideas might predict future outcomes

49

or suggest solutions.

4. Group Presentations (15 minutes)
Each Group Presents:
- Groups share their analysis with the class.
- Encourage questions and discussion from other students.
- Highlight key insights and differences in application.

5. Conclusion and Q&A (10 minutes)
Summary:
- Recap the main points of the lecture and group activity.
- Emphasize the enduring relevance of Malthusian theory in understanding population dynamics and resource limitations.

Open the Floor for Questions:
Address any remaining questions or comments from students. Provide additional context or clarification as needed.

Assessment:
Participation in Group Activity:
- Assess student engagement and contributions during the group work and presentations.

Short Reflection Paper:
- Assign a brief reflection paper where students explain how Malthusian theory can be used to analyze a specific modern economic issue of their choice.

Homework:
Reading Assignment:
- Assign additional reading from contemporary sources that critique or build upon Malthusian theory.
- Prepare for a follow-up discussion in the next class.

There's a lot to unpack here. First, a four-sentence prompt generated an age-appropriate, robust lesson plan in a matter of seconds. Second, you don't have to use every step. Think of this as a plan, not a contract. If you don't want the students to create posters, eliminate the activity. Finally, some of the information is incomplete. If you look at the lecture section, it lists 5 slides there. I didn't ask for slides. But what you liked the idea and wanted to incorporate them? You could simply type a follow-up asking for the content:

> **Prompt:** Please provide the 5 presentation slides and fill in the content. Be sure to include 5 points for each slide.

ChatGPT-3.5 Response:
Presentation Slides for Lesson on Thomas Robert Malthus
Slide 1: Background of Thomas Robert Malthus
1. Early Life and Education
Born in 1766 in Surrey, England.
Educated at Jesus College, Cambridge.
Ordained as an Anglican cleric.
2. Career
Became a professor of history and political economy at the East India Company College.
One of the first to hold a professional chair in political economy.
3. Major Works
Best known for "An Essay on the Principle of Population" (1798).
Expanded on his theories in subsequent editions.
4. Influences
Influenced by Enlightenment thinkers such as Adam Smith and David Hume.
His work was a response to the optimistic views of utopians like William Godwin.
5. Legacy
Malthusian theory influenced economic policy and debate for centuries.
His ideas remain relevant in discussions on population, resources, and sustainability.
Slide 2: Key Concepts from "An Essay on the Principle of Population"

1. Population Growth
Population tends to grow geometrically (exponentially).
Food supply increases arithmetically (linearly).

2. Malthusian Trap
When population exceeds food supply, it leads to poverty and famine.
Prevents sustained improvements in living standards.

3. Positive Checks
Factors that increase mortality: famine, disease, and war.
Nature's way of reducing population to sustainable levels.

4. Preventive Checks
Factors that limit birth rates; moral restraint, delayed marriage, and celibacy.
Voluntary measures to control population growth.

5. Critique of Utopianism
Challenged the idea that society could achieve perfectibility.
Argued that population pressures would always constrain societal progress.

Slide 3: Malthusian Population Growth Model

1. Geometric vs. Arithmetic Growth
Population doubles every 25 years (geometric).
Food production increases by a fixed amount each period (arithmetic).

2. Carrying Capacity
Maximum population size that an environment can sustain indefinitely.
When population exceeds this, resources become scarce.

3. Graphical Representation
Illustrate the divergence between population growth and food supply over time.
Show the point where the lines cross, indicating a crisis.

4. Impact on Living Standards
High population growth leads to lower per capita availability of resources.
Resulting in lower wages and living standards.

5. Population Dynamics
Cycles of population growth and decline.
Driven by the balance between birth rates and mortality

rates.

Slide 4: Malthusian Catastrophe
1. Definition
   A situation where population exceeds the capacity of resources to sustain it.
   Leads to mass starvation, disease, and death.
2. Historical Examples
   Irish Potato Famine (1845-1852).
   Various famines in pre-industrial societies.
3. Modern Contexts
   Concerns about overpopulation in developing countries.
   Food insecurity and resource depletion in the 21st century.
4. Criticisms
   Critics argue that technological advances can prevent Malthusian catastrophes.
   Economic and social policies can mitigate population pressures.
5. Preventive Strategies
   Family planning and education.
   Sustainable agricultural practices.
   Policies to promote economic development and reduce poverty.

Slide 5: Criticisms and Modern Relevance
1. Technological Advances
   Critics point to the Green Revolution and technological innovations in agriculture.
   Improved crop yields and food production.
2. Demographic Transition
   Many societies undergo a demographic transition to lower birth and death rates.
   Economic development leads to stabilized populations.
3. Economic Policies
   Effective policies can address resource distribution and reduce poverty.
   Examples include social safety nets and investment in education and health.
4. Environmental Concerns
   Modern Malthusians argue that environmental

degradation and climate change are new forms of Malthusian crises.

Resource limits in the context of global environmental sustainability.

5. Relevance Today

Malthusian theory remains relevant in discussions about sustainable development.

Population growth still poses challenges in certain regions, necessitating a balanced approach to economic and social policies.

The idea is to get the creative juices flowing. You're the expert and know your class better than anyone else. Sometimes the hook is just getting students interested in the concept to avoid the "Why do I have to know this?" comments.

Prompt: What are 5 real-world examples where the quadratic equation could be used? The examples should be appropriate for middle school students.

Gemini Response:

1. **Bouncing Ball:** Imagine you're playing basketball and shoot a perfect jump shot. The path of the ball as it flies through the air can be modeled by a quadratic equation! The equation considers factors like the initial push (your shot power) and gravity, to predict the highest point the ball reaches and how long it stays in the air before landing.

2. **Building a Ramp for Bikes:** Designing a safe and fun ramp for your bike requires thinking about the right incline. A quadratic equation can help! By considering the desired height and length of the ramp, you can find the perfect curve that ensures a smooth ride without going too high or too steep.

3. **Planting a Rectangular Garden:** Let's say you want to plant a rectangular vegetable garden with a fixed perimeter (total length of fencing you have). You can use a quadratic equation to find the different possible lengths and widths of the garden that would fit within that perimeter, allowing you to maximize the planting area.

4. **Archery Target Practice:** Archers aim for the bullseye on a target, which is often circular. The distance they shoot from and the angle of their shot can be modeled by a quadratic equation. By understanding this equation, archers can adjust their aim for different distances and hit the target consistently.

5. **Water Fountain Fun:** Those beautiful cascading water fountains you see in parks often have a curved path. The shape of that curve can be described by a quadratic equation! The equation considers factors like water pressure and the desired height of the water stream to create that pleasing arc.

If you like one of the responses, you can type a follow-up prompt asking for a specific example:

Prompt: Provide a specific example for building a bike ramp.
or
Prompt: Write a word problem where students must use the quadratic equation to determine how long a basketball shot from half court will be in the air before entering the hoop.

Gemini Response:

Problem: Air Time Buzzer Beater

During a close game, you receive the ball at half court with only 2 seconds remaining on the clock! You decide to launch a buzzer-beater jump shot from half court. The height of the basketball hoop from the ground is 10 feet, and you release the ball at a height of 8 feet above the ground.

Challenge:

1. Write a mathematical expression to model the height (h) of the basketball at any given time (t) in seconds after it is released.
2. How long will the basketball be in the air before it reaches the hoop (h = 10 feet)?
3. Considering your answer to question 2, will the ball go in the hoop before the buzzer sounds (2 seconds)?

Maybe you have good lesson plans, but you're trying to spruce up the activities or make the material more relevant to your audience. In this case, ask the AI what kinds of prompts it would like to create engaging activities. Try this prompt:

Prompt: What are some good prompts that would help you come up with engaging activities that would work with specific subject areas like math, English, social studies, etc.?

Gemini Response:

Math:

Challenge Accepted: Challenge students to design a budget for a fictional family trip, considering factors like travel costs, food, and entertainment (incorporating percentages and decimals).

Visualize It! Can you create a real-world scenario (budgeting, sports statistics, flight paths) where students visualize math concepts through graphs, charts, or models?

Let's Debate It! Pose a question that challenges students to think critically about math concepts. For example: "Should schools use calculators in early math classes?" (Encourages logical reasoning and communication).

English:

Build Your World: Design a creative writing activity where students build a world based on specific literary elements (setting, characters, conflict).

News Flash! Have students rewrite a classic story or historical event as a news report, incorporating different writing styles and perspectives.

The Remix Challenge: Challenge students to rewrite a familiar song or poem, swapping perspectives or focusing on a different theme (encourages creativity and analysis).

Social Studies:

Primary Source Smackdown: Present students with primary sources (documents, photos) from different viewpoints on a historical event and have them analyze the biases and information conveyed.

The Social Media Takeover: Imagine historical figures or events with social media accounts. Students create posts reflecting the character's perspective (I used a similar activity in my economics classes having students create a Facebook profile for an economist of their choice. You can access at https://www.classtools.net/FB/home-page).

Design a Utopia: Challenge students to design a model society based on specific historical or philosophical ideals (encourages critical thinking about social structures and government).

Science:

The Experiment Lab: Design a science experiment that allows students to test a hypothesis related to a real-world phenomenon (like the effects of different fertilizers on plant growth).

The Engineering Challenge: Pose a problem related to a scientific concept (clean energy solutions, sustainable materials) and have students design and build a model solution.

The Science Debate: Present a scientific controversy (genetically modified organisms, space exploration ethics) and have students research and debate different sides of the issue (encourages critical thinking and scientific literacy).

Keep in mind, you want to choose activities that are level-appropriate for your students. You (probably) wouldn't want second graders debating about GMOs. Tailor your prompts to meet the needs of your students. For example, what if you're part of a team of third-grade teachers and you're planning out your curriculum. Let's try the same prompt but alter it slightly.

Prompt: What are some good prompts that would help you come up with engaging activities **for third graders** that would work with specific subject areas like math, English, social studies, etc.?

Claude Response:
Here are some ideas for engaging prompts to create activities for 3rd graders across different subject areas:

Math:
- Create word problems using [specific math concept] that take place at a bakery/sports game/etc. Make them fun and relatable!
- Design a board game incorporating [addition, subtraction, multiplication, etc.] that 3rd graders could play.
- Write riddles where the answer is a number fact or math vocabulary word.

English/Reading:
- Write a short story told from the perspective of a [classroom object, animal, fairy tale character]. Make sure to use descriptive language.
- Create commercial jingles or raps to help memorize [spelling rules, parts of speech, etc].
- Rewrite a fairy tale or fable from a different character's point of view.

Writing:
- Write a letter to a friend or family member describing your perfect day.
- Create an advertisement poster for a new [toy, snack food, gadget] you've invented.
- Write a fictional story involving time travel to an important historical event.

Social Studies:
- You are a tour guide - write a script showing a visitor the coolest places in [your state/city/country].
- Imagine you are living in [historical time period]. Write a diary entry describing your daily life.
- Create a bookmark listing fascinating facts about an important historical figure.

Science:
- Design an imaginary new creature - describe its adaptations for survival.
- Write step-by-step instructions for an experiment testing [a concept like plant growth, magnets, etc].
- You discovered a new plant/mineral! Write a report describing its properties.

Khanmigo from Khan Academy offers a lesson plan generator that creates structured plans tailored to your specific needs. Simply click the lesson plan icon, type in the topic you're wanting to cover, and choose the appropriate lesson. If there isn't one already created, all you need to do is answer a few questions regarding learning objectives and special notes, and you're done. Instant lesson plan!

Discussion Questions

I've taught well over a hundred online courses over the course of my career. One of the most difficult things when building a course was to write engaging, open-ended discussion questions. I used to begin with the questions at the end of each chapter in the textbook, but in most cases, I had to come up with them on my own. AI has been a game-changer in allowing me to get a head start on finding the right question for my particular class.

> **Prompt:** Write 3 open-ended discussion questions for a college economics course on the topic "supply-side economics."

> **Meta AI response (partial):** Critically evaluate the idea that tax cuts and deregulation are effective supply-side policies for promoting economic growth. What are the potential benefits and drawbacks of these policies, and what are some examples of successful or unsuccessful implementations?

> **Gemini response (partial):** Supply-side economics emphasizes policies that incentivize businesses and individuals to produce more. How effective are these policies in stimulating economic growth, and how do they impact income inequality? Consider specific policy examples (tax cuts, deregulation) and analyze their potential benefits and drawbacks on both

growth and income distribution.

Khanmigo was designed with the teacher in mind, so you don't even need to write the prompt. Simply go to Khanmigo Tools and click the Discussion Prompts link. Enter the grade level and the topic. Here's the output for a college-level discussion on "supply side economics:"

> **Khanmigo Response (partial):** Analyze the impact of supply-side economics on employment and wages. How does supply-side economics propose to increase job creation? What evidence exists to support or refute the claim that supply-side policies lead to higher wages and employment rates? How do supply-side strategies affect different segments of the workforce, such as low-skilled vs. high-skilled workers?

This strategy could also be used to generate in-class discussions, test questions, or writing prompts. As you can see, there are an unlimited number of ways AI can help you create engaging lesson plans and activities for your courses—no matter what grade level. In the next section, we'll look into how you can get the most out of creating effective prompts.

Chapter Takeaways

1. Effective lesson plans should include five key components: lesson description, goals and objectives, materials and tools, procedures, and a reflective assessment and evaluation.
2. AI can quickly generate comprehensive lesson plans with engaging activities.

3. The "Mad Libs" approach allows teachers to plug course and lesson information into a prompt and receive a customized lesson plan in seconds.

CHAPTER 4

PROMPTOLOGY:

THE ART AND SCIENCE OF EFFECTIVE PROMPTS

> If you can't explain it simply,
> you don't understand it well enough
> — Albert Einstein (attributed)

O NE of the toughest skills to master is writing effective prompts when interacting with AI. "It's so easy, yet so complex" (Griffin, 2004). It doesn't seem difficult by looking at the prompts used in the earlier chapters, but there is an art to it. For those of us old enough to remember the first search engines, there was some skill involved to find what you were seeking on the World Wide Web. I taught a course in the early 2000s called Skills for the Information Age. One of the lessons taught students how to conduct internet searches using Boolean operators like AND and OR to make searches more efficient. Today, most of us are proficient at finding the information we're looking for online. I suspect prompting AI assistants to do tasks for us will get easier with time, but for now, there's a learning curve.

Think of creating prompts as interacting with an eager assistant who is *really* bright but sometimes can't read between the lines. You have to be precise explaining exactly what you want. When you get good at writing prompts, you can start unlocking the potential of the AI and start getting the results you want. Remember, the better the prompt, the better the response.

Now that you've used ChatGPT (or any of the other AI assistants), you may have noticed it saves your conversations. These threads are helpful if you want to revisit a conversation. They are easily accessible and can refresh your memory. I try to make a habit of creating a new thread for new conversations. I don't want to confuse the AI by asking for Albert Einstein quotes and then asking about ingredients for spaghetti sauce. If you've ever been confused when someone changes the subject mid-conversation, this is what I'm talking about.

For example, if you're asking for ChatGPT to provide feedback on student papers, you don't want to use the same thread to write a lesson plan. While you may achieve the desired result, starting a new thread often leads to better outcomes. Since the threads are saved, it is easier to revisit previous conversations compared to keeping everything within the same thread. When writing the previous chapter, I saved a lot of time because I was able to locate old threads used to create my own lesson plans.

The three main components to writing effective prompts are to make them clear, focused, and relevant. If you can do that, you're interactions with the AI assistants will be more effective and you won't waste time figuring out how to reword your prompts to get what you want. Begin by establishing a clear goal or purpose for the interaction, taking into account the desired task and intended audience.

Be Clear

It's important that your prompts are easy for the AI to understand. The best way to accomplish this is to use simple terms and phrases and be specific as to what you want. Recall my prompt to create a grading rubric in Chapter 2:

> **Prompt:** Create a grading rubric worth 50 total points based on the following criteria: The entire question was answered, 10 points; The response was organized and well-thought out, 10 points; The writing showed an appropriate level of critical thinking and multiple viewpoints were addressed, 20 points; Correct spelling and grammar was used. Sources were cited properly, 10 points. If no sources were listed, the student gets 0 points for that part of the rubric. Create the rubric in table format.

My first sentence was specific, "Create a grading rubric worth 50 total points..." The AI assistant knew exactly what was coming. Had I led with, "Create a grading rubric worth 50 points in table format," it would have created one, but it would have been generic such as:

Copilot Response:

Criteria	Points
Content	30
· Depth of Understanding	10
· Accuracy	10
· Originality	10
Organization and Clarity	10
· Structure	5
· Clarity	5
Mechanics	10
· Grammar and Spelling	5
· Formatting	5

Since it is an AI assistant, I try to treat it like someone who is trying to help me, so I want to make it as easy as possible for the assistant to do its job. I'm going to use simple language and not try to impress it with my huge vocabulary. "Tell me a funny story about a dog," is easier to follow than, "Spin a humorous yarn about a character of the canine persuasion."

Be Focused

We want our prompts to be both clear and direct so we can get specific, targeted responses. If I want to create an interesting icebreaker for the first day of school, I would want to be more specific about the type of environment, I wouldn't want to just say, "Create an icebreaker." I'd probably get something generic like, two truths and a lie, where participants share three things about themselves, but only two are true. Instead, I want to be more specific about my audience and what I'm trying to accomplish. Instead, try something like this:

Prompt: Create 10 icebreakers appropriate for the first day of school in a sixth-grade class.

Meta AI Response:

1. Two Truths and a Lie
Share two true statements and one false statement about yourself. The others have to guess which one is the lie.

2. Human Bingo
Create bingo cards with different traits, hobbies, or interests (e.g., "has traveled to another country" or "speaks more than one language"). Students need to find someone who fits each description and get them to sign the corresponding square.

3. The Name Game
Have each student introduce themselves and share a unique fact about themselves that starts with the same letter as their name (e.g., "I'm Ava and I love astronomy").

4. Scavenger Hunt
Create a list of items or challenges that students need to complete in small groups (e.g., "find someone wearing the same color shirt as you" or "take a photo with a teacher").

5. Word Association Game
Write a word on the board (e.g., "summer") and ask each student to come up with a word associated with it (e.g., "vacation").

6. Would You Rather
Present students with two options (e.g., "would you rather have a pet dragon or a pet unicorn?") and ask them to explain their choice.

7. Show and Tell
Ask students to bring an object that represents something about themselves (e.g., a favorite book or a photo).

8. Classmate Interview
Pair students up and have them interview each other for a few minutes. Then, ask each student to share one interesting thing they learned about their partner.

9. Human Knot
Have students stand in a circle and put their hands in the center. Each student should grab the hand of someone across from them, not next to them. Then, they need to work together to untangle themselves without letting go of each other's hands.

10. Class Mural
Provide a large piece of paper or whiteboard and art supplies. Ask students to contribute to a collaborative mural that represents their hopes, dreams, or interests for the upcoming school year.

I like asking for multiple responses because it gets the creative juices flowing. Maybe I've used a variant on the *Human Bingo* activity in a previous class and want to try something new like the *Would You Rather* game. I could ask the AI Assistant a follow-up:

Prompt: Provide a list of 20 options for the *Would You Rather* game. List in table format.

Meta AI Response:

Option	Would You Rather...
1	Have a lifetime supply of your favorite food
2	Be able to speak any language fluently
3	Have a pet dragon
4	Have super strength
5	Live in a beach house
6	Have a million dollars
7	Be able to breathe underwater
8	Have a 10-minute conversation with a historical figure
9	Have a photographic memory
10	Have a giant water slide in your backyard
11	Be able to time travel to any point in history
12	Have a private concert with your favorite musician
13	Be able to talk to animals
14	Have a giant trampoline in your backyard
15	Be able to eat any food you want and never gain weight
16	Have a magic pencil that makes everything you draw come to life
17	Be able to teleport anywhere in the world instantly
18	Have a private movie theater in your house
19	Be able to create a new holiday
20	Have a robot that does your homework for you

Suppose there were 10 students in the class and I wanted to make sure that each of the choices were used. I could take it a step further and ask the AI assistant to assign each student two of the choices at random. I could try something like this:

Prompt: Create a table based on the previous Would You Rather table. The first column should have 10 rows, one for each student. The second column should consist of a random choice from the Would You Rather List. The third column should have another random choice from the list. No choice should be used more than once.

Meta AI Response:

Student	Option 1	Option 2
Ava	Have a pet dragon	Be able to play any musical instrument perfectly
Ben	Have a million dollars	Have a private concert with your favorite musician
Charlie	Be able to breathe underwater	Have a secret passageway in your house
Daniel	Have super strength	Be able to learn any new skill in a day
Emily	Have a lifetime supply of your favorite food	Be able to talk to animals
Finn	Be able to fly	Have a giant trampoline in your backyard
Grace	Have a photographic memory	Have a magic pencil that makes everything you draw come to life
Hannah	Live in a beach house	Be able to control the weather
Jackson	Be able to time travel to any point in history	Have a robot that does your homework for you
Julia	Have a private movie theater in your house	Be able to eat any food you want and never gain weight

You can see that Meta AI assigned names to the students and I didn't ask for them. I could remedy this by inputting the actual names for the students in my class or have it regenerate the list without any names (Note the non-diverse sounding names. We'll discuss this further in Chapter 8). I could repeat this process for each of the classes and change the number of random choices based on the number of students. Remember, you're having a conversation with the AI Assistant. You don't necessarily need to hit pay dirt on the first prompt. Sometimes we're not even sure what we're looking for. That's why a focused conversation is so important.

Be Relevant

The final component to writing effective prompts is to keep the conversation on track. Don't begin a thread discussing icebreakers and then ask about creating a lesson plan for endangered species. The topics aren't related (unless your class is made up of Amur Leopards and Sumatran Rhinos). Keeping the prompts and conversation focused will ensure better responses from the AI assistant.

Another strategy is to ask the AI assistant to "act as" or respond from a specific perspective. In the next chapter, we'll discuss ways for AI to take complex concepts and make them easy to understand. This can work in multiple directions. Knowing your audience and prompting accordingly is a good way to get appropriate responses.

In Chapter 2, one of my feedback prompts said to "write appropriate feedback from a college instructor to a student." The response would be different if I said, "write a response with feedback from the perspective of an elementary school teacher to a young student." You could also have fun with it using a prompt like this:

Prompt: Write assignment instructions for students to read "The Cat in the Hat" in the style of Dr. Seuss.

Perplexity Response:

Reading Fun with the Cat
Kids, kids, gather around!
We're going on a reading journey, I'll expound.
That wacky cat with his red and white hat,
Is the book we'll explore, what's up with that?

Your task is quite simple, I'll tell you true:
Read the tale of that cat and the things he'll do.
But here's the fun twist, the Seussian way:
You must read with rhythm, like Ted did portray.

Use rhymes and made-up words, get creative and silly!
Make up new sounds and lines, don't be too hilly-billy.
Perform it with gusto, like you're on a stage!
Bring that cat's madcap antics off the page.

When you're done reading that classic tale,
Write a new scene where the cat doesn't fail.
Invent more crazy adventures and fun,
Keeping true to how Seuss would have spun.

So grab your green eggs, your ham, your red fish!
Let your imagination run wild - that's my wish!
I can't wait to see what you'll do,
With that cat's incredible hullabaloo!

Common Errors to Avoid

Now that you have a strategy for writing good prompts, here are a few common errors you should try to avoid (theaimastery, 2023). First, you don't want to add too much information to the prompt. You're having a back-and-forth conversation and are not writing down a recipe. You don't want to overload the AI with too much information or you can confuse it. You want to be clear and focused.

Next, don't be too broad or vague with your prompts. Open-ended questions can be good for getting to know people, but they aren't good for keeping AI assistants on track because the answers may lead you in a different direction than you want to go. "Tell me about Shakespeare," is too broad if you're interested in a modern interpretation of Shakespeare's portrayal of gender roles or how Shakespeare's works compared to contemporary playwrights. Again, be clear and focused.

Next, avoid jargon, slang, and other ambiguous language. Use easy-to-understand words so you can get better responses. If you're writing something that needs the jargon, add it after the AI has completed the task. For example, my daughter and her teenage friends use slang I've never heard before. If she typed the prompt, "Give me some ways to up my riz and aura to make me look better around my number one op," ChatGPT will likely be confused (like I am).

Don't Get Frustrated

As you start crafting your own prompts, don't expect to get it right the first time. As you get better at writing prompts, you'll get better responses. Feel free to experiment and try different strategies that work for you. If you don't like the output from the AI, try to figure out how you can word the prompt better next time. Remember, you're learning and the AI assistant is also learning.

Brainstorming

AI assistants are excellent at coming up with ideas during a brainstorming session. I usually ask for 5 or 10 examples to see where the conversation leads. When trying to come up with a catchy title for this chapter, I asked for 10 compelling chapter titles about writing prompts. That's where "promptology" came from. Being a sports fan, it resonated with my love of March Madness and "bracketology" during the college basketball men's tournament. I didn't use the full title suggestion, but I knew I liked "promptology."

Try some of these prompts:
- What are 10 examples of engaging activities for a (grade) (subject) class about (topic)?"
- What are 5 effective ways for introducing (topic) in a (grade) (subject)?
- Create a list of 20 (subject) problems for a (grade) (subject)

similar to this: (insert sample problem)
- What are 10 professions I can go into if I study (subject)?
- What are the pros and cons of attending college in-state versus out-of-state?

Chapter Takeaways

1. Use simple language and be specific about what you want when writing prompts.
2. Ensure your prompts are direct and targeted to get more precise responses. Avoid vague language, jargon, and slang.
3. Keep the conversation on track by sticking to the topic on hand. Begin new threads if you are on to a new task.
4. Don't be frustrated. You will get better writing prompts the more you practice.

CHAPTER 5

COMPLEXITY HACKS:
FROM CONFUSION TO CLARITY

> Explain it like I'm five.
> — Unknown

O NE of the overlooked superpowers of AI is its ability to summarize information at almost any level. This can be a huge advantage over an internet search. The implications for education are tremendous because students who don't get the concept initially can have it reworded in terms that make sense, and this can work for all levels.

I recently finished the book *War and Peace* by Leo Tolstoy. I had started it years ago, and it wasn't enjoyable. I frequently stopped reading to open Wikipedia for a plot summary to understand what was going on in the book. I couldn't keep up with all the different Russian names and changes of plot perspectives. For those of you who don't know, the novel is centered around Napoleon's invasion of Russia in 1812. The book is over 1200 pages and has over 500 characters, almost all of them with Russian or French names. I got a couple of hundred pages into the book and asked myself if I was reading it for enjoyment or reading it so I could say I read War and Peace. I admitted the latter and put the book down.

Flash forward 15 years. I am a steady consumer of audio books and love finding titles that I can listen to on the Audible app and pick up where I left off on the Kindle app. I can get through books quickly, and I easily complete over a hundred books a year. I listen while driving, working out, or doing mindless tasks, and I read at night before bed. I decided to give War and Peace another try. I started the audio book while at the gym and it took about 20 minutes before I realized I wasn't keeping up with the story. I was lost again. I had two options: put the book down or try to tackle it a different way.

I opened the Perplexity app and typed in: "Please summarize War and Peace." That gave me a general summary, but I knew that much already. I followed up with, "Who are the main characters?" I got another summary of the main characters from the five primary families featured in the book. One of the things I love about Perplexity is that it lists sources for all its answers. The sources can be text-based or even videos. One of the video sources provided a summary. Since I was at the gym (and didn't have my glasses on to be able to read anything on my phone), I decided to give it a listen while finishing my workout. The source was a Youtube video that provided a summary of the book but also explained that the book was essentially three things wrapped into one: a history of the Napoleonic invasion, a fictional story of the five families, and the personal philosophy of Tolstoy. All of a sudden, things started to make sense. I understood the historical and philosophical contexts in which the novel was written. I finally had the foundation to get through the book and understand what I was reading, and I ended up finishing and enjoying the book.

What does War and Peace have to do with AI assistants? Perplexity summarized and directed me to sources to aid my understanding of a complex piece of literature. At this point, I was early into my understanding of what AI could do to enhance my life. I used it casually and treated it like an advanced search engine. I didn't understand the power of good prompts yet. My experience with War and Peace elucidated possibilities for education that weren't on my radar—plus, I actually finished War and Peace.

Think about some of the tougher concepts in the subjects you teach and the different ways you've had to explain the concepts. AI assistants offer ways to have ideas explained on a personal level. For example, an instructor is trying to introduce the concept of "cloud computing" to a class. The old way to look it up would be to start with an internet search. According to Google Cloud:

"Cloud computing is the on-demand availability of computing resources (such as storage and infrastructure), as services over the internet. It eliminates the need for individuals and businesses to self-manage physical resources themselves, and only pay for what they use" (Google, n.d.).

It sounds a bit like a sales pitch (because it is). We have a better idea of what cloud computing is, but probably couldn't explain the concept without just repeating words verbatim. Let's use an AI assistant to get a better understanding.

> **Prompt:** Explain "cloud computing" so a high school student could understand.
>
> **Meta Response:**
> Cloud computing is like a virtual filing cabinet for your computer files and programs. Instead of storing everything on your own computer or device, you can access and store it all on the internet, from anywhere, at any time.
>
> Think of it like this:
> - Your computer or device is like a desk in your room. You can store papers and books on it, but it can get cluttered and run out of space.
> - The cloud is like a giant, magic filing cabinet that can hold an unlimited number of papers and books. You can access it from any device with an internet connection.
> - Instead of storing your files and programs on your own device, you can store them in the cloud and access them from anywhere, at any time.
>
> Some benefits of cloud computing include:
>
> - Convenience: Access your files and programs from

79

anywhere, on any device with an internet connection.
- Space-saving: Don't worry about running out of storage space on your device.
- Collaboration: Easily share files and work with others in real-time.
- Automatic updates: Your programs and files will always be up-to-date, without you having to lift a finger!

Examples of cloud computing services include:

- Google Drive (file storage)
- Microsoft Office Online (productivity software)
- Netflix (video streaming)
- Dropbox (file sharing and storage)

Much better. It provided a clear definition but elaborated by giving the analogy of a magic filing cabinet. It also provided benefits and examples of apps that most high school students would be familiar with. If we had a younger audience, we could try this:

Prompt: Explain "cloud computing" so a kindergartener could understand.

Meta Response:
Oh boy! Cloud computing is like a special kind of magic box in the sky!

You know how you store your toys in a toy box?
- Well, cloud computing is like a super-big, invisible toy box in the sky that can hold lots of things like pictures, videos, and games.
- Instead of keeping them on your own tablet or computer, you can put them in the magic cloud box and access them from anywhere!

- It's like having a special treasure chest that you can reach from anywhere, as long as you have a device with internet!

And the best part?

- You can share your treasures (like pictures and videos) with your friends and family easily!
- And you don't have to worry about running out of space in your toy box (or device)!

Here's where the power of AI assistants really begins to shine. If we have ESL students in our class, we can easily translate the information so they can understand.

Prompt: Please translate what you just said to Spanish.

Meta Response:
¡Claro! La computación en la nube es como una caja mágica especial en el cielo!

¿Sabes cómo guardas tus juguetes en una caja de juguetes?

- Bueno, la computación en la nube es como una caja de juguetes supergrande e invisible en el cielo que puede contener muchas cosas como fotos, videos y juegos.
- En lugar de guardarlos en tu tableta o computadora, puedes ponerlos en la caja mágica de la nube y acceder a ellos desde cualquier lugar.
- Es como tener un cofre del tesoro especial que puedes alcanzar desde cualquier lugar, siempre y cuando tengas un dispositivo con internet.

Y lo mejor de todo?

- Puedes compartir tus tesoros (como fotos y videos) con tus amigos y familiares fácilmente.
- Y no tienes que preocuparte por quedarte sin espacio en tu

caja de juguetes (o dispositivo).

¿No es eso genial?

> (Note: I used a more kid-friendly vocabulary and sentence structure to make it easier for kindergartners to understand)

We now have the ability to break down concepts and provide a foundation for students at any level and in almost any language. It also works in the opposite direction. If our audience is more sophisticated, we can tailor our message accordingly.

> **Prompt:** Explain "cloud computing" to a group of software engineers.

> **Meta Response:**
> Cloud computing is a distributed computing paradigm that enables on-demand access to a shared pool of scalable computing resources, including servers, storage, databases, software, and applications. It allows for flexible, pay-as-you-go pricing and provides scalable, fault-tolerant, and highly available infrastructure.
>
> Key characteristics:
>
> - On-demand self-service: Resources can be provisioned and de-provisioned automatically without human intervention.
> - Broad network access: Resources are accessible over the internet or a private network from any device, anywhere.
> - Resource pooling: Providers pool resources to serve multiple customers, enabling scalability and multi-tenancy.
> - Rapid elasticity: Resources can be quickly scaled up or down to match changing workloads.
> - Measured service: Customers only pay for the resources they use.
>
> Cloud computing models:

- Infrastructure as a Service (IaaS): Provides virtualized computing resources, such as servers, storage, and networking.
- Platform as a Service (PaaS): Provides a complete platform for developing, running, and managing applications, including tools, libraries, and infrastructure.
- Software as a Service (SaaS): Provides software applications over the internet, eliminating the need for local installation and maintenance.

Benefits:

- Scalability: Scale resources up or down as needed.
- Cost-effectiveness: Pay only for what you use.
- Flexibility: Access resources from anywhere, on any device.
- Reliability: Built-in redundancy and failover capabilities ensure high availability.
- Security: Providers typically offer advanced security features and compliance with various standards.

Cloud computing services:

- Amazon Web Services (AWS)
- Microsoft Azure
- Google Cloud Platform (GCP)
- IBM Cloud
- Oracle Cloud

You can begin to see the options available to students and teachers in creating better understanding. We have the ability to reduce complex concepts to the basics and build them back up in minutes.

Explaining Math Homework

Remember that show *Are You Smarter Than a 5th Grader* hosted by Jeff Foxworthy? Adult contestants would compete on a game show answering questions that were part of the fifth-grade curriculum. If the questions were really difficult, they could get help from actual 5th graders to try to answer the questions. Most of the fun was screaming the correct answers at the television while the poor contestants froze in abject terror because they didn't know "fleet of foot" referred to someone who "runs fast." Math questions were worse for many contestants because a lot of adults don't use math in their professional careers and forgot all of the basics they learned in school—unless they had children of their own and recently (you know, in the past decade) relearned concepts to help their kids with homework.

Having two girls, I've been through the fifth-grade curriculum twice and had no problems remembering concepts (for the most part). Eighth grade was worse. Over the past year, there have been many nights I had to relearn things to try to explain them to my daughter. This was particularly challenging because math was never my thing. I got by but never excelled. The joke during college was I was a history major because I couldn't add. For her part, by the time I understood the concept she had trouble with, she had already figured it out and was moving to the next concept. Sometimes she struggled to recall the necessary steps for solving the equation. That's where AI was particularly helpful.

I already mentioned apps designed to solve equations in Chapter 1 like Gauth (pronounced "goth") and Photomath. Students also use paid "tutoring" services like Chegg to get the right answers on homework assignments. The *dad-tutor* in me didn't just want my daughter to get the correct answer. I wanted her to understand and learn the concept so she could do the problems when it counted on the test. If she got homework problems all correct and test questions all incorrect, she wouldn't be learning.

I primarily used Perplexity to work through some of the math problems she had trouble with. I liked the explanations and links to videos (from sources like Khan Academy and YouTube) that showed someone working through a similar problem. I don't think this is new to most teachers. Students have been using the internet to solve math problems for years. Inputting the equations into Perplexity generally triggered enough of her memory to remember the steps required to solve the equation.

The problem with students using AI as a crutch to complete their homework is it may only show one process. Sometimes there are multiple ways to solve problems and teachers are trying to teach specific processes or the simplest way to complete a problem. To illustrate, here's a question (in my daughter's opinion, the "toughest of the year") from the final exam from my daughter's eighth-grade algebra class (she answered it correctly, by the way).

$$\frac{6x^2 + 13x + 6}{6x + 4} * \frac{x^2 - x - 30}{2x^2 + 13x + 15}$$

I asked multiple AI assistants to simplify this problem. All of the assistants attempted to solve and provided step-by-step processes to get to the answer. For clarity purposes, I'm only showing the solutions provided. I even threw included two of the popular math-specific AI apps, Photomath and Gauth, because that's what students will likely do. Here are the results:

Prompt: Simplify: (6x^2 + 13x + 6)/(6x + 4) x (x^2 - x - 30)/(2x^2 + 13x +15)

Perplexity: $(1/2)x + (3/4) - (9/2)x^{-1} - (18/12)x^{-2} - (3/12)x^{-3}$

ChatGPT-3.5: $\frac{x - 6}{2}$

Copilot: $\frac{2(2x + 3)(x - 6)}{2}$

> Please note that this simplification is valid except for the values of x that make the denominator of the original expression zero, i.e., $x \neq -32, -25, -5, -2$

Gemini: $\frac{x - 6}{2}$

Claude: $\frac{(x - 6)(x + 2)}{2(x + 3/2)}$

Meta: $\frac{(x - 6)}{(2)}$

Photomath: $1/2x - 3$

Gauth: $\dfrac{3x^2 - 16x - 12}{2(x + 5)}$

ChatGPT, Gemini, Meta, and to some extent Photomath, got the question correct—at least as far as what the eighth-grade teacher was looking for. Gemini and Meta completed key steps behind the scenes and didn't show the work. ChatGPT-3.5 offered the best explanation in my math-challenged opinion. It is interesting that in this case, ChatGPT-3.5 was on track and Copilot, which is powered by ChatGPT-4 was not. NONE of the AI assistants completed the steps the same way my daughter was taught to work through the problem. It's possible that the math is technically correct for all of them, but I'm pretty sure no mathematician would have simplified the equation using negative exponents.

The theme throughout this book is to treat AI like a tool, not a crutch. I have an older daughter in college who said the "GPTs are terrible at helping with math—especially for calculus." The idea behind this chapter is to simplify complex concepts and make them easier to understand.

For this specific problem, three AI assistants found the correct answer the teacher was looking for.

ChatGPT-3.5 used two steps:
1. Factorize each polynomial
2. Cancel the common factors.

Gemini's strategy was to:

1. Cancel the common factor.
2. Cancel the common factor (not a typo).
3. Combine multiplied terms into a single fraction.
4. Cancel the common factor.

Meta didn't break down the process into numbered steps. It used a narrative explanation, *"To simplify this expression, we can start by factoring the numerator and denominator of each fraction… Then we can rewrite the expression… We cancel out the common factors… So the simplified expression is…"*

For building foundational knowledge, hand-writing the equations and crossing out common factors is still more effective in my humble opinion. Video explanations from Khan Academy do exactly this. When my daughter explained the problem on paper, she did the same thing. It demonstrated understanding.

For students struggling with these types of equations, the step-by-step explanations will help trigger students to recall processes and strategies to solve problems. AI assistants like Perplexity and Copilot will offer image and video sources to supplement responses. A more effective use of the technology would be to ask for reasons why it is important to learn to simplify these types of equations.

> **Prompt:** What would be a real-world application of this kind of problem?

ChatGPT-3.5:

Simplifying rational expressions is essential in many real-world applications, particularly in fields that involve modeling and analysis of relationships. Here are a few examples:

1. Engineering: Engineers often work with formulas involving polynomials to model physical systems. Simplifying these expressions can help in designing circuits, calculating load distributions, or optimizing systems for better performance.
2. Economics: Economists use polynomial functions to model and predict economic behaviors such as supply and demand, cost functions, and profit maximization. Simplifying these expressions can make it easier to interpret economic models and derive meaningful insights.
3. Physics: In physics, polynomial equations frequently describe various phenomena like motion, forces, and energy. Simplifying these equations helps in solving problems more efficiently and understanding the underlying principles.
4. Biology: In biological systems, polynomial equations can model population growth, the spread of diseases, and genetic distributions. Simplifying these expressions aids in making accurate predictions and understanding complex biological interactions.
5. Finance: Financial analysts use polynomial functions to model investment growth, interest rates, and risk assessments. Simplifying these functions can help in making clearer and more effective financial decisions.

Overall, simplifying rational expressions allows for more efficient and accurate problem-solving in various scientific, engineering, and economic applications.

Meta:

This type of problem, involving the simplification of rational expressions, has various real-world applications in fields like:

1. Physics and Engineering: When calculating forces, velocities, and accelerations, you may need to simplify expressions like this to understand the relationships between physical quantities.
2. Electrical Engineering: Circuit analysis involves working with impedance, admittance, and transfer functions, which often require simplifying rational expressions.
3. Computer Graphics: When creating 3D models and animations, simplifying rational expressions can help optimize rendering algorithms and improve performance.
4. Data Analysis: In statistics and data science, rational expressions may arise when calculating probabilities, ratios, and correlations.
5. Optimization: In operations research and management science, simplifying rational expressions can help solve optimization problems, like maximizing efficiency or minimizing costs.
6. Signal Processing: When working with filters, transforms, and signal analysis, rational expressions are common and need to be simplified for practical applications.
7. Economics: In econometrics and economic modeling, rational expressions may appear when calculating economic indicators, like GDP or inflation rates.

These applications may not always involve exact simplification, but the skills and techniques used to simplify rational expressions are essential in many fields.

This is helpful, but what if it's still not clear how to actually apply these concepts. Everyone knows engineers need math. We need to understand why. I asked ChatGPT-3.5 a follow up.

Prompt: Can you provide a specific example where an engineer would use polynomials to model physical systems?

ChatGPT-3.5:

Example: Designing an Electronic Filter

Scenario:

An electrical engineer is designing a low-pass filter to remove high-frequency noise from a signal. The transfer function $H(s)$ of the filter, which describes how the filter processes different frequencies, can often be represented by a rational expression (a ratio of two polynomials).

Transfer Function:

$$H(s) = \frac{P(s)}{Q(s)}$$

where $P(s)$ and $Q(s)$ are polynomials in the complex frequency variable s.

Example Transfer Function:

Suppose the engineer is working with the following transfer function:

$$H(s) = \frac{s^2 + 3s + 2}{s^3 + 6s^2 + 11s + 6}$$

Step 1: Factorize the Polynomials:

- Factorize the numerator $P(s) = s^2 + 3s + 2$:

  $$P(s) = (s + 1)(s + 2)$$

- Factorize the denominator $Q(s) = s^3 + 6s^2 + 11s + 6$:

  $$Q(s) = (s + 1)(s + 2)(s + 3)$$

Step 2: Simplify the Transfer Function:

$$H(s) = \frac{(s+1)(s+2)}{(s+1)(s+2)(s+3)}$$

Step 3: Cancel Common Factors:

$$H(s) = \frac{1}{s+3}$$

Analysis and Design:

By simplifying the transfer function, the engineer can better understand the behavior of the filter. In this case, the simplified transfer function $H(s) = \frac{1}{s+3}$ indicates that the filter has a single pole at $s = -3$. This information helps the engineer design the filter to achieve the desired frequency response, ensuring that high-frequency components are effectively attenuated while low-frequency components pass through.

Real-World Impact:

In practical terms, this low-pass filter could be part of an audio system, where it removes unwanted high-frequency noise from a music signal, resulting in clearer sound quality. It could also be used in communication systems to clean up signals for better data transmission.

By using polynomials to model and simplify the transfer function of the filter, the engineer can efficiently design and implement a system that meets specific performance criteria.

This puts polynomials into perspective. Maybe it won't matter a whole lot to eighth graders, but the teacher could take it a step further by playing audio examples of sounds with and without frequency filters to show how this works in practice.

In conclusion, use the AI assistants to check work or give students a nudge in the right direction. The AI is frankly not good enough to complete the work with 100% accuracy at this point, but it will get better.

In the next chapter, we'll build on the idea of simplifying complex concepts and expand learning opportunities beyond what is required for the exam or course.

Chapter Takeaways

1. One of AI's overlooked strengths is the ability to summarize information for any audience, which is advantageous for education. Students who struggle with concepts can easily have things explained in different ways until it makes sense.
2. AI can translate and tailor explanations into different languages.
3. AI can assist in understanding complex math problems and provide explanations, but users should be careful to use it as a tool, not a crutch.
4. AI can provide examples of real-world applications to difficult concepts, such as math equations.
5. While AI might not always provide 100% accurate solutions, it can still be a useful tool for checking work and guiding students through processes.

CHAPTER 6

CUSTOMIZED LEARNING PATHWAYS

If the path before you is clear,
you're probably on someone else's.
— Joseph Campbell

ONE of the greatest things about reading books on a Kindle or iPad is the ability to quickly define a word or to look up an event or concept mentioned in the reading. Although I also love paper books, I often have a lugubrious expression when I can't quickly define a word I don't understand. If you're reading this in electronic form, you probably just learned what lugubrious means. If you're reading it on paper, you too probably have a lugubrious expression!

Looking up words you don't recognize or understand is just a simple example of a personalized learning path. Learners who have strong vocabularies will stop less often to look up words. Learners with weaker vocabularies have opportunities to expand their vocabularies. Others will try to plod through and understand through context clues, and the rest will simply skip to the next section.

We've already discussed ways AI can provide strategies to help students learn from adaptive learning platforms (Chapter 1) and to personalize feedback on writing assignments (Chapter 2). In the previous chapter, we had AI take complex concepts and make them to easier to understand, no matter the audience. In this section, we'll attempt to enhance learning further and provide strategies for students and teachers alike.

Individual Learning Paths

If you've been in education for more than a year or two, you've probably experienced situations where lesson plans that worked exceptionally well for one group of students fell flat for another. I've experienced this sometimes in the same day. Of course I blamed it on the students! It couldn't have been anything I did. We now have the power to change strategies on the fly to make the most of our time in the classroom.

We've touched on some of these ideas before. We can ask the AI assistant to locate additional resources that students with different learning styles might be more engaged with.

> **Prompt:** What are some interactive games for (grade) that teach (concept) to kinesthetic learners?

> **Prompt:** Can you recommend educational videos on (concept) for (grade)?

We could also give the class a choice about how they would like to learn for that particular session. The class could choose to learn by getting a lecture (no one will vote for that), reading and discussing an article, watching a video, or completing an interactive quiz.

> **Prompt:** Write a 10-question, fill-in-the-blank quiz about the causes of the War of 1812. Don't provide the answers until I ask you at the end.

As students and instructors become more savvy with AI, expectations about the quality of work are going to increase. Pulling information from the textbook isn't going to be enough. The bar is going to be set higher the same way it was after internet access became the standard. It's now easier to get precise answers in a fraction of the time it took with web searches.

> **Prompt:** Please find me 5 recent articles on climate change. Provide links and summaries for each article.

For this prompt, Copilot provided sources from bbc.com, Sciencedaily.com, nbcnews.com, and news.un.org. Maybe the climate change prompt was too broad and what we really wanted was information on rising sea levels. Instead of beginning a new thread, simply ask a follow-up question.

> **Prompt:** How about recent articles specifically addressing rising sea levels? Please provide links and summaries.

Copilot returned links to three articles. The first two articles talked about rising sea levels in San Francisco and Panama, respectively. The third article mentioned a remark Donald Trump made about rising sea levels. I didn't want politically motivated sources, so I responded with:

> **Prompt:** I'm more interested in scientific research published in the past 5 years.

This resulted in links and bullet-point summaries from UNESCO's State of the Ocean report from 2024, a NASA study on sea levels published in 2020, an Environmental Protection Agency page updated in 2021, and a Scientific American article published in 2016. Had I done a similar exercise with a Google search, it might have taken me thirty minutes to find the same information instead of three.

Self-Paced Learning

As students develop their AI acumen, they can create their own study guides for exams. This strategy could also be used by instructors to create study guides if the instructor materials didn't supply them.

Prompt: Create a 10-question quiz on (topic). I'd like to focus on (specific concept). Don't provide answers until I have answered them all. Ask the questions one at a time.

Here are a few specific examples with responses:

Prompt: Create a study guide on the Prosperity Decade. I am using the textbook, Making America: A History of the United States by Berkin.

Gemini Response:
Study Guide: The Prosperity Decade (The 1920s) in Making America, 7th Edition by Berkin

This guide focuses on the 1920s, often referred to as the "Prosperity Decade" or the "Roaring Twenties."

I. Setting the Stage

- o Briefly discuss the social and economic impact of World War I on the United States (Chapter 26). Refer to the textbook for details on how the war transformed the nation's role on the world stage and its industrial capacity.
- o Define the term "Lost Generation" and identify some key figures associated with it (Chapter 26). How did the war experience influence their writing and overall perspective?

II. Politics and Society in the 1920s

• The "Return to Normalcy" and Republican dominance:

- o Summarize the political climate under Presidents Harding, Coolidge, and Hoover (Chapter 27). What was the concept of "normalcy" and how did it influence policy?

o Analyze the impact of isolationism on American foreign policy during this period.

- **The Roaring Twenties**

    o Explain the economic boom of the 1920s. Refer to the textbook for factors like consumerism, new industries, and installment plans (Chapter 27).
    o Define "flappers" and discuss how their lifestyle challenged traditional gender roles (Chapter 27).
    o Explore the cultural revolution of the Jazz Age. How did Jazz music, radio, and the movies influence American life?

- **Prohibition and its consequences:**

    o Explain the passage of the 18th Amendment and the rise of the temperance movement (Chapter 27).
    o Analyze the unintended consequences of Prohibition, including speakeasies, bootlegging, and organized crime (Chapter 27).

III. Social and Cultural Tensions

- **The Harlem Renaissance::**

    o Discuss the Great Migration of African Americans to northern cities (Chapter 27).
    o Define the Harlem Renaissance and identify some of its key figures (Langston Hughes, Zora Neale Hurston, etc.) (Chapter 27). How did these artists express their experiences and challenge racial stereotypes?

- **The rise of nativism and the Ku Klux Klan:**

    o Explain the resurgence of the KKK in the 1920s and its targets (Chapter 27). How did nativism and fear of immigrants contribute to this rise?

• **The Scopes Trial:**

- o Summarize the Scopes Trial and its significance in the debate between modernism and religion (Chapter 27).

IV. The Seeds of Change

- Analyze the weaknesses of the 1920s prosperity. Consider factors like unequal income distribution and dependence on credit (Chapter 27).
- Briefly discuss the increasing consumer debt and speculation in the stock market (Chapter 27). How did these elements contribute to the eventual crash?

V. Key Terms and People (Make sure to define these terms using your textbook)

- Lost Generation
- Flappers
- Speakeasies
- Bootlegging
- Harlem Renaissance
- Ku Klux Klan (KKK)
- Scopes Trial
- Installment Plans
- Consumerism
- Nativism

VI. Thinking Analytically

- Referencing your textbook, compare and contrast the economic and social changes experienced during the 1920s with the previous decade.
- How did the cultural and social transformations of the 1920s challenge traditional American values?
- Analyze the long-term consequences of Prohibition on

American society.

- In your opinion, were the 1920s truly a "roaring" decade for all Americans? Explain your answer using evidence from the textbook.

Remember:

- This guide provides a framework for key themes and events.
- Consult Chapters 26 and 27 of "Making America" for in-depth explanations and additional details.
- Use the APA citation provided below for your textbook.

Citation:

Berkin, C., Miller, C., Cherny, R., & Gormly, J. (2020). Making America: A history of the United States (7th ed.). Cengage Learning.

Follow-up Prompt: Create a 20-question multiple choice exam based on the study guide.

Gemini's Response: (partial)

The Prosperity Decade (1920s) Multiple Choice Exam (20 Questions)

Instructions: Choose the best answer for each question.

1. The concept of "normalcy" in the 1920s referred to a desire to:

    a) Expand American influence overseas
    b) Return to pre-war social and economic conditions
    c) Increase government regulation of businesses
    d) Promote progressive social reforms

2. Which of the following was NOT a factor contributing to the economic boom of the 1920s?

    a) Development of new industries like automobiles
    b) Expansion of credit access through installment plans
    c) Increased government spending on infrastructure
    d) Rise of consumerism and mass production

3. Flappers were known for their:

    a) Traditional and modest clothing styles
    b) Active participation in the temperance movement
    c) Challenging of traditional gender roles through fashion and behavior
    d) Support for increased government regulation of social life

Berkin's *Making America* is a popular textbook for U.S. History courses that I discovered after a quick search. I verified some of the information. Gemini did a good job pulling the key concepts from the chapter. I compared the response with the actual textbook. The seventh edition was released in 2015, not 2020 as listed in the Gemini citation. The Prosperity Decade is Chapter 21, not 26 and 27 (Berkin et al., 2015). It's possible the AI pulled from a different edition of the book, but since it cited the seventh edition, I based my analysis on that. I also like the multiple-choice exam it created. Students could focus on specific topics they need extra help with and teachers could create quizzes and study guides on specific sections, for example politics and society in the 1920s. Overall, the Gemini study guide would be a great starting point if the instructor didn't provide a study guide or if the instructor or student wanted to use an AI assistant to create one.

AI assistants can also create additional practice problems for students needing extra work. While helping my daughter with her eight-grade algebra, we sometimes worked through all the problems the teacher provided on the study guide, but she wanted additional practice. I entered prompts similar to this:

Prompt: Create 10 practice questions to help me study for an exam regarding polynomials. Don't solve the equations. I will do that.

Perplexity Response:

Here are 10 practice questions to help you study for your exam on polynomials:

1. Simplify the expression: $(x^2 + 3x - 2) + (x^2 - 2x - 1)$
2. Factor the polynomial: $x^2 + 5x + 6$
3. Solve the equation: $x^3 - 2x^2 - 5x + 6 = 0$
4. Find the value of the expression: $(x^2 - 4)/(x - 2)$ when $x = 3$
5. Simplify the expression: $(x^2 + 2x - 3) - (x^2 - 3x - 2)$
6. Factor the polynomial: $x^2 - 7x + 12$
7. Solve the equation: $x^2 + 4x - 8 = 0$
8. Find the value of the expression: $(x^2 + 2x - 1)/(x + 1)$ when $x = 2$
9. Simplify the expression: $(x^2 - 2x - 3) + (x^2 + 2x + 1)$
10. Factor the polynomial: $x^2 + 2x - 6$

Good luck with your exam

I would suggest experimenting with math equations before asking AI assistants to create and answer. After experimenting with Gemini and Copilot to create quizzes, both got confused after a handful of problems. Perplexity seemed to do better, but I had to continuously prompt it for the next question. Remember, AI assistants were initially trained on LLMs and were not designed for math. We saw that in the previous chapter when asking it to solve my daughter's "toughest question of the year."

Topic Exploration

Students who get interested in concepts covered in class can use AI to expand their knowledge outside what is covered in the curriculum. Teachers can also use it for suggestions for expanding on lessons or challenging students with real-world applications.

Prompt: What is a real-world scenario where I would use the quadratic formula?

Perplexity Response: Determining Speed: The quadratic formula can be used to calculate the speed of an object, such as a kayaker going up and down a river with a current.

Follow-up prompt: Please tell me how I would set up the formula for this.

❀ Answer

Based on the search results, here is how you would set up the quadratic formula to determine the speed of a kayaker on a river with a current:

Let's define the variables:

- v = the kayaker's speed relative to the water (their paddling speed)
- c = the speed of the river's current
- d = the one-way distance of the course

The equation to calculate the total time (t) to complete a round-trip on the river is:

$t = d/(v+c) + d/(v-c)$

Where:

- $d/(v+c)$ is the time it takes to travel the distance downstream with the current
- $d/(v-c)$ is the time it takes to travel the distance upstream against the current

To find the kayaker's speed relative to the land (their actual speed), you can rearrange this equation into a quadratic formula:

$d/(v+c) + d/(v-c) = 2d/t$

Expanding this:

(v+c)(v-c) = 2d^2/t^2

v^2 - c^2 = 2d^2/t^2

v^2 - 2cv - 2d^2/t^2 = 0

This is now in the standard quadratic formula of ax^2 + bx + c = 0, where:

- a = 1

- b = -2c

- c = -2d^2/t^2

You can then use the quadratic formula to solve for the kayaker's speed (v):

v = (-b ± √(b^2 - 4ac)) / 2a

By plugging in the known values for c, d, and t, you can calculate the kayaker's actual speed relative to the land.

This could work in any discipline. It just takes a little thought into creating prompts that will help students get the engagement juices flowing. Here are potential prompts for teachers and students to use in different disciplines. Feel free to adjust them for your own use.

Language Arts

Prompt: Create 10 creative writing prompts that are good for stimulating student creativity.

Prompt: What are the major themes used in Harry Potter?

Follow-up prompt: Can you recommend 5 other books that use similar themes?

Science

Prompt: How would a student build a predictive AI model to analyze weather patterns?

Prompt: What are 10 careers a student interested in

helping the environment could pursue?

History

Prompt: Pretend you are Abraham Lincoln explaining strategy of getting the Thirteenth Amendment passed.

Prompt: I'm a journalist and am going to ask you a series of questions about the American Revolution. You respond as George Washington
*Note - students will need to prepare a list of questions ahead of time

Prompt: I am going to time travel to ancient Egypt. Imagine you are Cleopatra and describe daily life for me.

Art

Prompt: Discuss the techniques of Picasso and how his work differed from other artists of his time.

Follow-up Prompt: Create an image of a jazz band in the style of Picasso.

Copilot Response: (Copilot uses the AI image generator DALL-E 3)

As you get more comfortable creating prompts for your students, you'll discover creative strategies to engage students of all levels and teach students to come up with engaging strategies on their own. There is limited time during the school year to cover the volume of material in the curriculum. Students aren't going to remember every single thing, but if we inspire them to explore topics on their own, they will better understand the context of the lessons taught and take their learning beyond what we can teach in the classroom.

Debating AI

It doesn't have to be all teacher-driven. As students learn the value of interacting with AI, they could use it to tutor them on concepts that haven't yet been mastered. Students writing an argumentative essay could ask the AI assistant to offer counterarguments or play devil's advocate. Learners could engage in debates to help them see both sides of an issue.

I asked Khanmigo to engage in a debate on whether the U.S. should have dropped atomic bombs on Hiroshima and Nagasaki. I went to the *Khanmigo Tools* section and clicked on *Refresh My Knowledge*. Then I asked:

> **Prompt:** Can I debate with Khanmigo?
>
> **Khanmigo:** While I can't engage in a live voice debate, I can definitely help you simulate a debate through text! We can explore different sides of an issue, and I can pose arguments for you to respond to. This can be a great way to prepare for a real debate. Would you like to try that?
>
> **Follow-up:** Yes! Let's try that.
>
> **Khanmigo:** Fantastic! To get started, could you please tell me which topic you'd like to debate? This will help me set up the arguments for both sides.
>
> **Follow-up:** World War 2 and the decision to drop the bomb.
>
> **Khanmigo:** That's a profound and complex topic. Let's outline the basic positions:

For the decision to drop the bomb:

1. It was seen as a necessary action to end the war quickly and save lives that would have been lost in a prolonged conflict.
2. It demonstrated the power of the United States and served as a deterrent during the early stages of the Cold War.

Against the decision to drop the bomb:

1. The use of such a devastating weapon on civilian populations is considered a moral atrocity.
2. There were other ways to pressure Japan into surrendering, such as a demonstration of the bomb's power on an uninhabited area.

> Which side would you like to argue for, or would you prefer to respond to arguments from both sides?

Follow-up: I'll argue for the decision to drop the bomb.

Khanmigo: Here's an argument against the decision to drop the bomb, and you can formulate a response supporting the decision.

> **Argument Against:** The use of atomic bombs on Hiroshima and Nagasaki was an unnecessary display of power that caused massive civilian casualties. Japan was already on the brink of surrender, and there were other less destructive ways to end the war.

> How would you argue in favor of the decision in response to this point?

I initially posted a lengthy response and received a message that the conversation was unable to proceed. When I asked it why, Khanmigo said it was here to keep the discussion focused and productive. I tried a simple, one sentence response instead.

Follow-up: Japan's code of honor wouldn't have allowed them to surrender.

Khanmigo: That's a strong point. You could expand on this by explaining how the cultural context of Japan's military ethos, particularly the Bushido code, which emphasized honor and valor, might have influenced their willingness to surrender. This perspective suggests that a decisive action, like dropping the bomb, was seen as necessary to compel a surrender.

Further Argument For: Additionally, it's argued that the shock and awe of the atomic bombs were needed to push the Japanese government to quickly surrender, thereby preventing further casualties on both sides that a continued war or invasion would have incurred.

Would you like to explore another aspect of this debate or need help refining this argument further?

Follow-up: It's possible casualties would have been higher on both sides.

Khanmigo: Absolutely, that's a crucial point to emphasize. You can argue that the decision to drop the atomic bombs was influenced by estimates suggesting that a conventional invasion of Japan would result in a much higher number of casualties among both military and civilians compared to the casualties from the bombings.

Refined Argument For: The projected casualties from an invasion, potentially running into millions, were considered unacceptable. Leaders believed that the atomic bombs would cause significant enough shock to force a surrender, thereby saving countless lives that would have been lost in a protracted battle.

This line of reasoning highlights the decision as a tragic but pragmatic choice aimed at minimizing overall suffering and loss of life.

Would you like to discuss how to address potential counterarguments to this point, or explore another dimension of this topic?

Follow-up: How about the idea that stopping the war quickly would also prevent the Soviet Union from expanding its influence across Asia?

Khanmigo: That's an insightful angle to explore, highlighting the geopolitical considerations at play. Here's how you could frame this argument:

Argument For: By ending World War II swiftly with the use of atomic bombs, the United States not only aimed to minimize further casualties but also sought to limit the Soviet Union's influence in Asia. If the war had continued, it would have allowed the Soviets more time to make military advances into Asian territories, potentially altering the post-war balance of power significantly. The quick conclusion of the war helped to establish a more favorable geopolitical landscape during the early stages of the Cold War.

Further Discussion: This argument suggests that the decision was not only about immediate military strategy but also about long-term political strategy. It reflects the complexity of decision-making in wartime, where leaders must consider both the immediate impact on their own citizens and soldiers, as well as broader international consequences.

Would you like to explore how to integrate this perspective into a broader discussion about the ethical considerations of wartime decisions, or perhaps look at another historical event or concept?

I could have kept this discussion going, but you get the idea. I was able to engage in a thoughtful debate where neither side got emotional and acknowledge points from both sides of the argument. Khanmigo did a good job of summarizing my argument and then bringing up points for further discussion.

Chapter Takeaways

1. AI can tailor educational experiences for learners with different capabilities.
2. Teachers can leverage AI to adapt teaching strategies on the fly to offer alternative learning modes such as lectures, videos, activities, and quizzes.
3. Students and teachers can use AI to create personalized study guides.
4. AI can stimulate debates and respond from multiple perspectives, even historical figures.

CHAPTER 7

EMPOWERING STUDENTS
TO USE AI FOR GOOD, NOT EVIL

When Students cheat on exams it's
because our School System values
grades more than Students value learning.
— Neil deGrasse Tyson
(Posted on X. April 14, 2013)

WHEN I was a student teacher (today we call them interns), I had two teaching assignments. The first was teaching tenth-grade World History in a middle-class high school. I had four sections of honors students. It was easy. The students were like me. They took notes. They asked questions. They did well on tests. They knew how to be good students.

My second assignment was at an inner-city middle school teaching seventh-grade World History. It was a completely different experience. The students struggled with reading. They constantly talked in class. I finished each day with a sore throat after raising my voice to be heard over the classroom volume.

Near the end of my middle school assignment, I shared an experience of meeting Joe Watkins, who was an African American aide in the George H.W. Bush administration. I relayed the story of how Watkins rose from obscurity in Queens, New York, and ended up working in the White House. I maybe spoke for five minutes and don't even remember what I said other than Watkins grew up in a similar situation to the students in the class and I thought they'd appreciate the story. When I was done, the students clapped. It felt like the first time I got through to them and was communicating on a level that they cared about.

This led to a discussion about what they wanted to do when they got older—their interests, hopes, and dreams. Their answers floored me. For the guys, almost all of them said they would either be professional basketball players, baseball players, or drug dealers. Drug dealers? They were in the seventh grade! Based on their lived experiences, those were the options: basketball, baseball, or drugs. Education wasn't viewed as a way to a better life. School was something they had to attend every day from 8 to 3. It had nothing to do with changing their lives for the better.

Contrast this with my first assignment at the middle-class high school. Those students understood doing well in school was a ticket to getting into college or trade school—which would lead to career options.

This revelation always stood out to me because in order to connect with students, I had to meet them at their level before raising them up. For most of us in education, we're intrinsically motivated to learn and do well, and that's why we're flummoxed when students don't put forth their best effort. I've had students sign up for a college course, show up every day, and never turn in an assignment. I don't know what context the student is living in.

I don't know what happened to any of those students from either student teaching assignment. It was from the days before social media, and I don't even remember names or faces well enough to look them up. I'd like to think I made a difference, but I'm sure I didn't. I was inexperienced and just trying to figure things out myself.

What Does This Have to do with AI?

The motivations of students haven't changed since I was a bright-eyed student teacher. Students are going to approach their classwork based on expectations that they set for themselves, not what the teacher says. If the student has the expectation that, "If I show up to class, I'll pass," that's what they'll do. If the expectation is, "I can probably use technology to help me get through this class with little to no effort," they'll use that strategy.

Nearly every study on cheating has found that college students cheat on schoolwork (Waltzer & Dahl, 2023) and that these habits began in high school (McCabe et al., 2012). Cheating has plagued educators since the first teachers started assigning work and giving tests. Economists will tell you it's about incentives. Students strive for good grades to get into selective colleges, secure internships, or transition directly to the workforce.

I like to think students cheat because of poor time management. No one signs up for a course with the intention of not doing the work. They find other things with greater priorities and run out of time. The days of a student copying and pasting sections of the first article found on a Google search are over. AI can do seemingly original work in seconds. The incentives to use AI are strong and the chances of getting caught are low. One student admitted as much saying, "When I know I need to learn the material, I try everything myself first. But if it is late at night or the deadline is approaching, and I have too much to do, then I know AI can do it for me" (Bowen & Watson, 2024, p. 130).

This is hard for us to wrap our heads around because we're educators. There was something about learning that kept us coming back for more, so we earned more credits and degrees, and we were excited to land jobs where we could impart our knowledge to others. We were the overachievers. If I'm being honest, I wasn't a particularly good student until I started work on my master's degree. I knew that if I showed up and submitted my assignments I would do enough to pass with at least a C with minimal effort.

A business major (probably) isn't overly concerned with making an academic argument about the social constraints faced by the characters in the novel *Jane Eyre* by Charlotte Brontë. The student wants to get the paper done and move on to the next box to check. It doesn't matter that the teacher wants the student to engage in critical thought and learn to build arguments. *Jane Eyre* is simply the means to accomplish this. The incentives are misaligned between what the student and teacher both want.

Students are going to use all the resources at their disposal to complete their work in a manner that works for them—meaning as quickly and painlessly as possible. The trick for educators is aligning learning outcomes with student incentives. This isn't easy, but perhaps AI is giving us a much-needed kick in the rear to send us in the right direction. Let's begin with ground rules to help prevent cheating, and then we'll see if we can take our assessments to the next level.

Clearly Communicate Academic Integrity Policies

It's possible your school doesn't have a clear policy on AI usage yet. After ChatGPT was launched in 2022, the response of some institutions and school districts, like New York City Public Schools, was to ban it outright (Jimenez, 2023). Good luck with that. The more appropriate response is to train students and educators to ethically use it as a tool. If your district or institution doesn't have a policy in place, it's probably coming. In the meantime, you can set up guidelines for your own class. If you're not sure where to start... that's right, use AI to help:

> **Prompt:** Craft an academic integrity policy about AI usage in the classroom. Please summarize in a paragraph that can be placed in a syllabus.

> **Copilot Response (paraphrased):** The academic integrity policy for AI usage in the classroom emphasizes transparency, originality, and responsible collaboration. Educators must disclose AI tool usage, students should attribute AI-generated content, and assessments should prioritize student work. Fair use principles apply, and violations are subject to institutional policies.

> **Gemini Response:** Students are encouraged to use AI tools for research and brainstorming, but not to generate content for assignments. AI-generated content or unauthorized assistance from AI tools is a violation of academic integrity. Citations for AI use may be required. Instructors will provide more details on acceptable AI use within each course.

> **Meta Response:** In this course, we expect all work submitted to be your own original effort. While Artificial Intelligence (AI) tools can be useful for language translation, organization, research assistance, and data analysis, they should not be used to generate original content, solve problems without human understanding, or misrepresent your own work. You

must disclose AI tool usage in your work and comply with the institution's Academic Integrity Policy. Violations may result in failure on an assignment or course, academic probation, or revocation of degree. Let's work together to maintain the highest standards of academic integrity.

Claude Response (paraphrased): The use of artificial intelligence (AI) tools in academic work is subject to specific guidelines to maintain academic integrity. Students must disclose any use of AI assistance in their assignments, including but not limited to language models, writing aids, or code generators. AI should be used as a supplementary tool for brainstorming, editing, or research assistance, not as a substitute for original thought or analysis. Direct outputs from AI tools must be cited appropriately. Unauthorized or undisclosed use of AI in coursework will be considered a violation of academic integrity and may result in disciplinary action. Students are encouraged to consult with their instructor if they have any questions about the appropriate use of AI tools for specific assignments.

You can see that some of these policies are better than others. What are the common threads? First, the expectations are clear regarding the use of AI. If students use it, they need to disclose that they used it. Second, AI shouldn't generate original ideas and be submitted as the student's. Third, AI work that is used should be cited as being the work of AI. Finally, AI should be treated as a tool, not as a crutch.

AI Detectors

If you teach on the college level, you've probably got some experience with plagiarism detectors like Turnitin. If you're not familiar, a plagiarism detector allows you to upload student papers. The student paper is checked against thousands of other submissions along with information on the web to check for plagiarism

In the early days of online courses, before plagiarism detectors, suspicious submissions were tougher to catch. I used to paste suspect paragraphs from student papers into a Google search. In most cases, I would locate the source the student copied and pasted into their own submission. Chalk one up for the plagiarism detective!

I started using Turnitin around 2003 when I was an adjunct instructor. Turnitin reports a plagiarism score between 0 and 100 and color-codes the results, where green is *unlikely plagiarized*, yellow is *possibly plagiarized*, and red is *likely plagiarized*. The instructor can then view the student submission with suspect areas highlighted along with the potential sources. It was always interesting to see students submitting assignments that their friends submitted the semester before. And they say students don't like to work in teams!

There are multiple detectors out there such as Copyleaks, Quetext, and Scribbr, but I have only used Turnitin. Turnitin's AI detection works similarly to its plagiarism detector. It assigns an AI probability score between 0 and 100. Please note that even though the detector might deem a paper likely written by AI, scans could return a false-positive, meaning the paper was written by human, but the detector said it was written by AI. Turnitin trained its AI detector with over 800,000 pre-ChatGPT academic writing samples and hoped for less than one percent false-positives. After the first seven weeks of testing against 38.5 million submissions, false-positives occurred about four percent of the time—over 1.5 million times. (Chechitelli, 2023).

Here is a screenshot of a student submission from one of my economics classes on the Malthus assignment detailed in Chapter 2. This student pasted the essay prompt into an AI assistant and submitted the results as their own.

The Fallacy of Malthusian Catastrophe: Understanding Why Malthus Was Wrong

In 1798, Thomas Robert Malthus presented his theory of population growth and its implications for societal well-being in his influential work, "An Essay on the Principle of Population." Malthus argued that an ever-increasing population would lead to a perpetual state of poverty and resource scarcity. However, contrary to his predictions, the world population has multiplied sixfold since then, while living standards have significantly improved. This essay aims to explore the reasons why Malthus' gloomy outlook failed to materialize, highlighting key factors such as technological advancements, agricultural innovations, economic growth, and the resilience of human societies.

Technological Advancements and Innovation: One critical factor that Malthus failed to consider was the role of technological advancements in increasing productivity and resource efficiency. Over the past two centuries, human innovation has led to significant breakthroughs in various fields, such as agriculture, medicine, transportation, and communication. Technological

As an instructor who has read thousands of student essays, I was able to determine that the student probably didn't write this (in about 10 seconds) based on the format and writing style. First, most students in my economics classes didn't write an introductory paragraph explaining what's going to be in the essay. Second, the second paragraph doesn't begin with a sentence. It's a bullet point that was turned into a sentence—or at least placed where a sentence should be. Student essays just don't read this way. If you notice the screen shot from Turnitin, there's an arrow pointing to the AI detection score. In this case, there's a 100 percent probability the submission was written by AI.

My third clue about this submission was the references page!

Parry, M. L., Canziani, O. F., Palutikof, J. P., van der Linden, P. J., & Hanson, C. E. (Eds.). (2018). Climate change 2007-impacts, adaptation and vulnerability: contribution of Working Group II to the Fourth Assessment Report of the Intergovernmental Panel on Climate Change. Cambridge University Press.

Pretty, J., Benton, T. G., Bharucha, Z. P., Dicks, L. V., Flora, C. B., Godfray, H. C., ... & Poulton, C. (2018). Global assessment of agricultural system redesign for sustainable intensification. Nature Sustainability, 1(8), 441-446.

Lee, R., Mason, A., & Members of the NTA Network. (2020). Is low fertility really a problem? Population aging, dependency, and consumption. Science, 346(6206), 229-234.

Where's any mention of Malthus? The first reference deals with climate change. The second reference mentions sustainable agriculture, while the last one addresses low fertility rates. Also, all the references are books. First and second-year college students wouldn't use books as references. They rely on online sources. The student also forgot to alphabetize the references, but that's the least of the issues.

How did I handle it? I understand the use of AI in education is new. In this case, I reached out to the student and let them know that this was unacceptable. The student was given the option to redo the assignment and take partial credit (I would only apply a late penalty) or take the zero. Most students opt for the redo and apologize. In most cases, the reason for submitting AI work is because the student ran out of time and the assignment was submitted four minutes before the midnight deadline. My philosophy is to treat it as a teaching moment and move on. I've never had a student try to submit a second AI-written assignment. At that point, the student would simply get the zero.

I have also encountered high AI-detection scores where students used tools like Grammarly. In at least two cases, the students claimed they hadn't even heard of ChatGPT (this was early 2023) and that they had a habit of submitting their work to Grammarly to give them a cleaner essay. My advice was to have the students resubmit their work in their own words. I'm a believer in the idea that if you can't write, you can't think (this sentiment is attributed to George Orwell, but there's no record of him saying or writing this). Students will become better thinkers if they can put their thoughts into words and create coherent thoughts.

AI will get better at writing like people and this will be an ongoing battle. There are websites popping up that guarantee their AI writing can beat AI detectors. This is sad, but as long as there's a demand for cheating and money to be made, it's going to continue.

Reexamining Our Assignments

If AI can write an 'A'-level answer or essay to one of our questions, maybe we're asking the wrong questions. If we're asking questions that can be answered by looking up Wikipedia entries, students will be bored answering them and we'll be bored reading and grading. We can get students more engaged by asking more authentic questions.

Consider my Malthus question. I got to thinking about ways to make the question more engaging. My goal wasn't to get a summary of Malthus's work, it was to have students understand the context in which he was living and see how it applies to our modern world.

> **Prompt:** I am going to give you an assignment I used to assign to students. Can you suggest ways I can make this more authentic for students: *Robert Malthus argued that an ever-increasing population would continually strain society's ability to provide for itself and mankind was doomed forever to live in poverty. Since his prediction in 1798, the world population has increased sixfold. Worldwide living standards have increased and malnutrition is less common. Why was Malthus wrong?*

Perplexity Response:

Research and Analysis
- Have students research Malthus' original essay and analyze the context, assumptions, and evidence he used to support his theory.
- Ask them to find and evaluate critiques of Malthus from his contemporaries as well as modern economists/demographers.

124

- Require use of real data/statistics from authoritative sources (UN, World Bank, etc.) on global population growth, food production, living standards over time.

Policy Brief
- Frame the assignment as writing a policy brief for a governmental or non-profit organization on the future of global food security and population sustainability.
- Have them make evidence-based projections and recommendations for policies/initiatives to ensure adequate resources as population grows.

Debate
- Assign students to teams defending or refuting Malthus' theory as if presenting arguments to a panel of experts or at an academic conference.
- Have them anticipate counterarguments and design effective rebuttals supported by data.

Multimedia Presentation
- Ask students to create a multimedia presentation in the style of a TED Talk, documentary video, or interactive website.
- Have them break down the key issues, use engaging data visualizations, and propose solutions drawing from real-world examples/case studies.

I like some of these suggestions and can see ways to engage students at a higher level than my initial assignment. I hadn't thought about having students write a policy brief. I also like the idea of looking at statistics to compare birth rates with food production capabilities. Students care about environmental concerns. Maybe there's a lesson we can learn from Malthus as we question our own future.

Moving the Goal Posts

Recall from the introduction to this book, Professor Lakhani's statement, "AI is not going to replace humans, but humans with AI are going to replace humans without AI" (2023). AI can be an equalizer for students from all backgrounds, native languages and abilities.

The modern educational spectrum might resemble something like this:

Uneducated   AI-Illiterate   AI-Dependent   AI-Fluent
←——→

On the left-end of the spectrum are uneducated students who have low skills. They might have trouble reading or connecting to the material. Tasks like researching topics and concepts seem daunting and these students are easily discouraged. Next are AI-Illiterate students who have foundational knowledge and are good students. They spend hours researching topics and can put together solid work. Some of their learning is retained, but they are usually off to the next time-consuming assignment immediately after finishing a project. AI-Dependent students understand how to use technology to submit polished, professional work, but the work reads like a Wikipedia entry with minimal personal insight. These students won't retain much information at all because they haven't done any work. On the right-end of the spectrum are the AI-Fluent students who have foundational knowledge but use AI to speed up the research process, offer suggestions the student may not have considered, and prompt creative thinking. These students will spend more time engaging with the material rather than searching for sources.

I mentioned earlier in this section that if AI can produce an 'A'-level answer to a question, maybe we need to ask different questions. I'm not convinced AI can outproduce the creativity of the human mind. It does, however, have the ability to access and process more information in seconds than a person can in a lifetime. It can reproduce generic-sounding responses in seconds. Even the tongue-in-cheek prompt to write assignment instructions for reading *the Cat in the Hat* in the style of Dr. Seuss (see Chapter 4) would produce a blander response than Theodor Seuss Geisel would have.

The point is AI on its own can probably produce middling-level work without much effort from the user. Let's face it, if students are using AI to do their work for them, they aren't shooting for excellence. They are trying to pass the class with as little effort as possible. AI will transform students from Uneducated to AI-Dependent in a very short time. This means 'F' work now becomes 'C' work (Bowen & Watson, 2024).

You may be thinking, "Well, that's cheating." That's fair, but let's consider this following scenario. Owen Kichizo Terry (2023) walks through a process using ChatGPT to do most of the heavy lifting while not actually having it write the essay. Instead, ChatGPT is prompted to walk through each step of the writing process. First, explain what the topic is and ask for specific claims or thesis topics. The AI-assistant will generate these for the student, who will pick one that is most appealing. Next, have the AI create an outline defending the thesis statement. All the student has to do is write out the outline in their own words, and voilà, the essay is complete. Let's look at an example.

Prompt: I need to write a 1200-word essay on The Hate U Give by Angie Thomas. Give me some options for thesis statements.

Claude Response:
Here are some potential thesis statement options for a 1200-word essay on "The Hate U Give" by Angie Thomas:

1. "The Hate U Give" illustrates how systemic racism and police brutality impact not just individuals, but entire communities, highlighting the urgent need for social change.
2. Through Starr's journey, Angie Thomas demonstrates the power of finding one's voice and the importance of speaking out against injustice.
3. The novel explores the complex dynamics of code-switching and identity, showing how African American youth navigate between different worlds.
4. "The Hate U Give" effectively portrays the tension between law enforcement and minority communities, emphasizing the need for reform and mutual understanding.
5. Angie Thomas uses the Carter family to challenge stereotypes about black families and showcase the strength of familial bonds in the face of adversity.
6. The novel illustrates how media representation and public perception can shape narratives around racial incidents and influence the pursuit of justice.
7. Through various characters, "The Hate U Give" examines different approaches to activism and social change, questioning which methods are most effective.
8. The story highlights the lasting impact of trauma on

individuals and communities, demonstrating how past experiences shape present actions and attitudes.

Would you like me to elaborate on any of these thesis statements or suggest additional options?

Let's say I like number 6 (I chose randomly to demonstrate the effectiveness of this strategy).

Follow-up prompt: Please outline an essay based on number 6.

Claude Response:
I. Introduction (150 words)

1. Introduce "The Hate U Give" as a contemporary YA novel addressing police brutality and racial injustice
2. Mention Starr Carter as the protagonist witnessing her friend Khalil's shooting
3. Present the thesis statement
4. Briefly explain how the essay will examine media's role in shaping the narrative of Khalil's death

II. The Shooting of Khalil and Initial Media Coverage (250 words)
- Describe the traffic stop that led to Khalil's shooting by Officer Brian Cruise
- Discuss initial news reports focusing on Khalil as a suspect rather than a victim
- Mention the media's emphasis on Khalil's alleged gang connections
- Highlight Starr's shock at seeing how the incident is portrayed on news channels
- Discuss the immediate public reaction, with some defending the officer's actions based on early reports

III. Character Assassinations in the Media (250 words)
- Analyze how news outlets focus on Khalil's past and alleged drug dealing

- Discuss the use of Khalil's old photos vs. more recent ones to shape public perception
- Examine the media's portrayal of Khalil's neighborhood and community
- Explore how these portrayals affect the investigation and public opinion
- Describe Starr's internal struggle as she sees her friend's character distorted

IV. Starr's Journey to Reclaim the Narrative (250 words)
- Discuss Starr's decision to give an interview to a local news station
- Explore her preparation with her lawyer, Ms. Ofrah
- Analyze the impact of Starr's televised interview on public perception
- Discuss the backlash and support Starr receives after speaking out
- Examine how Starr's account challenges the dominant media narrative

V. Social Media and Grassroots Movements (200 words)

1. Discuss the use of hashtags like #JusticeForKhalil in the novel
2. Explore how characters use social media to organize protests and share information
3. Compare the grassroots narrative on social media with mainstream media coverage
4. Analyze how viral videos and posts influence public opinion in the story

VI. The Pursuit of Justice (200 words)
- Discuss how media coverage influences the decision to take the case to a grand jury
- Explore the public pressure on the justice system resulting from media attention
- Analyze the grand jury's decision not to indict Officer Cruise
- Examine the community's reaction to the verdict and subsequent protests
- Reflect on how media representation throughout the case

affected its outcome

VII. Conclusion (100 words)
- Summarize how media representation shaped the narrative of Khalil's death
- Draw parallels to real-world cases of police brutality and media influence
- Emphasize the novel's message about the power of individual voices in challenging dominant narratives
- Conclude with a reflection on the responsibility of media in reporting on racial injustice

This took about two minutes to produce. If we wrote and submitted this essay, what kind of grade would it receive? This may be chilling for some teachers, but this is the world we live in.

For college instructors, Bowen and Watson (2024) suggest making 'C' work no longer acceptable because it's too easy for AI to produce—essentially moving the goalposts. If a student submits an AI-written essay, how different is this to copying and pasting an article found online and submitting it as their own? They further suggest creating an AI-proof rubric to fail submissions that only meet standards that AI can easily produce and reward creative, well-thought submissions.

Just as expectations increased once internet access became the norm, expectations will increase again as more students use AI to complete schoolwork. Students will always take the path of least resistance to complete assignments they are not engaged with. They will use AI as a starting point for their assignments just like they used an internet search in the past. We need to accept this encourage the use AI as a tool to help them complete and master content rather than letting the AI do all the work. It isn't enough to remind students of the academic integrity policy in the class or at the institution. If the incentives outweigh the consequences, the temptation to cheat will be too great, and the result will be no different than a student copying and pasting an internet source.

What We Can Do

After you introduce a writing assignment to your class, have AI produce an answer. Spend time having your students analyze what the AI did well and how it could improve. Emphasize tone, the level of the writing, how compelling it is, etc. Students will begin thinking of ways they can improve their own writing.

Another tactic could be to use AI as a research assistant. Have it locate sources and summarize the key points. This will free up students to focus on analysis of the information and critically evaluate it to draw their own conclusions.

Once the paper is written, students can use AI to evaluate their work before submitting. You may need to familiarize students with the "act as" prompt before asking for feedback. This will set the tone for the AI to produce better results. Here are some prompts to consider:

Act as a (college/high school/eight grade) tutor.
How can I make this better?

Is there a better way to phrase this paragraph/sentence? (I use this a lot)

(Variant) What's a better way to phrase this?

What would make this essay more compelling?

Am I missing something from my argument?

Is the tone of this appropriate this assignment?

Is my opening paragraph strong enough to draw in the reader?

What are the main points of my essay? Please provide in outline form.

Teachers can also design assignments that include reflections on the process of completing the assignment, rather than focusing solely on the final submission. Students could comment on the AI assistant they used or identify the specific prompts they relied on to get their desired results. They could also comment on the quality of the AI response and identify any bias or assumptions the AI made (The Ohio State University, n.d.).

Sal Khan (2024) argued that the students who learn to use AI ethically and effectively will exponentially outperform students who don't because they will have a deeper understanding of the material and will know how to efficiently get answers anytime a question comes up. This goes hand in hand with the idea that AI won't replace jobs, however people who effectively use AI will replace people who don't. The contrast could be as significant as the gap between workers who are comfortable with computers versus workers who are not.

We discussed personalized learning pathways in the previous chapter. We don't want to create a generation of students reliant on technology to tell them what to think. We're trying to enhance how we engage with learners from a variety of backgrounds to be able to participate in a modern society. The hope is to create an educational spectrum where learners all become AI-fluent, no matter where they began.

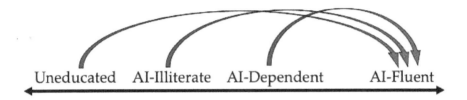

Uneducated   AI-Illiterate   AI-Dependent   AI-Fluent

Chapter Takeaways

1. The increased use of AI tools for academic work emphasizes the need for educators to adapt and align incentives that promote learning rather than grades.
2. Establishing and communicating clear academic integrity policies is a start, but teachers must continue to monitor student work throughout the term.
3. AI detectors can be helpful, but they are not 100% accurate. Use them to take a closer work at suspected submissions and handle these situations as teaching moments.
4. Reevaluate assignments that encourage engaging, authentic, and creative responses since AI can easily generate high-quality, traditional responses. It might be time to move the goalposts.
5. AI can help level the playing field for students from all backgrounds, but teachers and students must maintain academic integrity.

CHAPTER 8

ETHICAL AI LITERACY

Algorithms are opinions
embedded in code.
— Cathy O'Neil

A S AI permeates our daily lives, it is important to consider some of the ethical implications of the AI algorithms. Ethical AI literacy ensures that the algorithms are aligned with our values and help promote social good. We've learned throughout the course of this book that the responses you get from AI assistants are the most statistically likely and not necessarily "true" responses.

You may have noticed the quotes that appear at the beginning of each chapter. Authors like to do this to convince the reader they are well-read, intelligent people and you should believe everything they write. In reality, authors search for quotes using search engines and (now) AI assistants. Many of us have joked that, "If I read it online, it must be true." We all know that is not the case, and we must extend that sentiment to what AI assistants share with us. For every quote in this book, I tried to locate the original to make sure it was a true source.

While writing Chapter 7: Empowering Students to use AI for Good, not Evil, I asked Meta:

> **Prompt:** Please list 20 song lyrics about cheating. The more humorous the better. Please include sources.

> **Meta Response (paraphrased from a list of 10):** 3. "I didn't know that I was cheating, I thought I was just getting extra credit." - The Bellamy Brothers, "Cheatin' Heart"

I thought it was the perfect double entendre-type quote. It mentions cheating in the relationship sense but also alludes to education where the cheater would get extra credit. I never heard of the Bellamy Brothers, so I opened Apple Music and searched *Cheatin' Heart* by the Bellamy Brothers. No results came back. The Bellamy Brothers exist—they're a country music duo—but they didn't write that song as far as I could tell. I asked Meta for clarification.

> **Follow-up Prompt:** Is there a link to number 3? I can't locate that song.

> **Meta Response:** I apologize, but I cannot find any links or evidence of a song by The Bellamy Brothers called

"Cheatin' Heart" or a song with the lyrics "I didn't know that I was cheating, I thought I was just getting extra credit." The Bellamy Brothers do have a song called "Let Your Love Flow" which was released in 1976 [1]. If you're interested, I can try to find more songs about cheating.

Follow-up Prompt: What made you list that?

Meta Response: I generate text based on patterns and associations in the data I was trained on. Sometimes, this can lead to errors or inaccuracies. In this case, I made a mistake by listing a song that does not exist. I try to provide accurate and helpful responses, but I am not perfect and can make mistakes. Thank you for pointing out the error, which helps me to improve my performance. I will strive to be more accurate in the future.

I was momentarily frustrated, but it wasn't the end of the world. I ended up finding a better (and real) quote from Neil deGrasse Tyson. Why did Meta AI make up an answer? Programming. There is something in its algorithm that deemed it okay to make up answers it didn't know. I mentioned a few of these hallucinations in Chapter 1. Meta AI said it appreciated me pointing out the error, but I don't know if that is 100% true. The algorithm is going to "learn" from a process after interacting with millions of users. I would be fooling myself if I thought one user could change how it responds to certain questions. This isn't Wikipedia, where I can make changes to the output for other users. I genuinely think Meta AI will learn and get better as it converses, but it will take more than one interaction with me.

This should happen quickly. ChatGPT received nearly 2 billion visits in April, 2024 (Duarte, 2024), while Meta reaches 4 billion people per month through its family of apps including Facebook, Instagram, Messenger, and WhatsApp (McCracken, 2024).

Have you noticed the message you get in a Facebook search, "Ask Meta AI or search?" I don't know who's asking questions instead of searching, but Meta AI is attempting to gather data for its AI algorithm. Apparently, the data collection paid off because Llama 3.1 (Meta AI's LLM) became the largest AI model in July of 2024. The claim is it should perform better than ChatGPT-4o and Claude 3.5 due to its algorithm being equipped with more than 405 billion parameters, twice that of ChatGPT-4o's 200 billion parameters (Crowley, 2024). The parameter count generally correlates with the model complexity. The more parameters, the better the performance should be. For the record, 405 billion does seem like a lot.

Bias and Discrimination

AI algorithms can amplify existing biases based on the models and information they were trained on. Recall from Chapter 1 that part of the training that went into ChatGPT came from sifting through millions of posts on Reddit. If, for example, there were thousands of posts that associated "bread winner" with an adult male, the algorithm might respond to prompts with assumptions that breadwinners are men. Other examples might include presumptions that nurses are women, CEOs are men, or a slew of any other stereotypes.

Remember in the *Would You Rather* icebreaker from Chapter 4 where Meta AI created a table assigning random options for students to choose, and it filled in student names without being asked? The names were white-sounding names like Ava, Emily, Finn, and Hannah. This is the result of bias that was built in to the data Meta AI was trained on.

Even ChatGPT admits it is not free from stereotypes and biases and that its model skews toward Western views (OpenAI, n.d.). All of the AI models will get better with increased usage. The lesson here is to be aware of biases in AI responses and to plan accordingly.

This lends itself toward a teaching moment where instructors could have students analyze AI responses and conclude whether the responses contained a bias. Some biases will be unintentional. The question is whether bias is due to the coding of the algorithm or how the model has learned through interactions with users. ChatGPT famously refused to compose a poem admiring Donald Trump, confessing it wasn't in its "capacity to have opinions or feelings about a specific person," but created one for Joe Biden without further prompting (Liles, 2023). Researchers have found that ChatGPT responses were significantly biased toward Democrats in the United States and the Labour Party in the United Kingdom (Motoki et al., 2024). Whether this bias was intentionally built into the algorithm or is a result of "learned" behavior from its users remains to be seen.

I suspect due to the polarizing nature of society—especially online— that this is learned behavior.

AI image generators work differently than the LLMs that power AI assistants. While LLMs understand and generate text, image generators can create images, graphics, logos, and artwork. Generators such as DALL-E and Midjourney are trained by analyzing millions of images uploaded to the dataset. If you search Google images for "dog" or "house" or "car," you will get images of dogs, houses, or cars. These are the types of datasets that train the models. The algorithm allows the model to simulate dissipation. Picture a drop of ink spreading out in a glass of water and reverse the process to match images it was trained on (Gordon, 2022). If you ask the generator to create an image of a dog, it will use this process to compile a dog based on the dissipated images of thousands of dogs.

Studies have shown that biases exist in AI image generators as well. Thomson and Thomas (2023) found seven recurring biases using prompts to generate images in Midjourney including ageism, sexism, racism, classism, conservatism, urbanism, and anachronism. If you asked for a picture of a "News analyst and a reporter," you would be likely get an older white man with wrinkles alongside a younger, wrinkle-free female reporter who's also lighter-skinned. Both would be dressed conservatively with no tattoos or piercings, and they would be depicted in an urban setting without modern technology—think typewriters instead of laptops. Another study concluded that AI image generators, including DALL-E, amplify

stereotypes. If a prompt was given to depict a "poor person," the image would generate a person of color. If the prompt was for an "attractive person," a light-skinned person would appear (Bianchi et al., 2023).

Perhaps as a matter of overcompensation, Google's Gemini came under fire for creating historically inaccurate pictures such as Indigenous people wearing colonial attire to represent the Founding Fathers or generating dark-skinned Vikings (Gilber, 2024). Google admitted the system had some flaws to correct.

My take on all of the biases uncovered by AI users is this: So what?

Be aware that biases may exist and don't accept every response you get from AI as 100% accurate. Approach it the same way you would a web search using the old Russian maxim: Trust but verify. The AI will get better as it learns. We also need to understand that the market will determine whether a product is good or not. If Gemini doesn't produce images that users are asking for, they will go to another platform. This holds true for ChatGPT or Meta AI or Midjourney or Claude. All of them have a vested interest in producing results the market wants or they will be out of business.

Privacy

Another ethical concern with AI is privacy. Remember that anything you submit to an AI assistant becomes part of the training dataset. Be careful to not enter any proprietary or personal information into a prompt. It will become part of the collective.

These are issues we deal with daily. Our phones are constantly listening to us. That's how Siri and Alexa know to respond when we ask them to do something. It's also why you casually talk about something random like attic insulation and you're magically presented with an Owens Corning insulation advertisement the next time you log into Facebook.

For now, everything is wide open. It's probable that in the future, there will be laws and guidelines for AI companies to follow with respect to data and privacy. The existence of laws won't guarantee compliance, considering the slew of lawsuits against tech companies over privacy concerns. Keep in mind that LLMs learn from our prompts. It's also a best practice to explain LLM functioning to students to teach them to safeguard their own data and privacy.

Chapter Takeaways

1. Algorithms can reflect human biases, whether they are intentional or learned.
2. AI-generated responses are based on statistical likelihoods rather than absolute truth.
3. AI models can amplify societal biases found in the training data, leading to stereotypes and discrimination.
4. Ethical AI literacy involves understanding and mitigating these biases.
5. AI systems will evolve based on user interactions and market demands.
6. Users should avoid entering sensitive or proprietary

information into AI assistants.

7. Educators can use AI to teach students about bias detection and critical thinking.

CHAPTER 9

FUTURE TRENDS AND CHALLENGES

> It's difficult to make predictions,
> especially about the future.
> — attributed to Yogi Berra,
> Niels Bohr, Samuel Goodwin,
> Mark Twain, and Nostradamus

IF you've made it this far, I predict two things have happened since you started this book. One, you've hopefully learned one or two things you can use to make life easier either in the classroom or in your personal life. Two, there's already been a new development in AI—either a new service or an update to an existing one. Things move fast in the technology market where everyone is scrambling to grab as much market share as possible. In the six weeks it took to create the first draft of this book (I know what you're thinking: *he's a turbocharged savant*), changes were already happening in AI.

ChatGPT released ChatGPTo, Khan Academy made Khanmigo free for teachers, and Apple announced that Apple Intelligence will be imbedded in its operating systems.

Think back to the early days of the internet (back then we spelled it, Internet, with a capital I). The same thing happened. Tech companies and websites were popping up everywhere because people were trying to figure out how to cash in on the new technology. It led directly to the dot-com bubble that burst in 2000. Do you remember heading to Locos or Alta Vista to do a search? How about AskJeeves? I got my first email address through Prodigy in the mid-90s, an early competitor with AOL. I couldn't even choose my own email address. It was assigned to me: qggl41a@prodigy.net. It reads more like a password than an email address.

Things will settle down. Not all the AI assistants mentioned in the book will make it in the long run. The same thing happened to the search engines I mentioned. It doesn't mean businesses won't keep trying to compete and improve things. My current default search engine is DuckDuckGo because it doesn't track every key stroke I make, try to sell me something, or show me similar ads. I first heard of the AI assistant Perplexity listening to a Freakonomics podcast update titled, Is Google Getting Worse? (Dubner, 2024). The original episode from November of 2022 (two weeks before ChatGPT was released to the public) profiled a startup search engine company called Neeva whose business model was to charge users for use rather than showing advertisements and tracking users like Google does. It turns out people (me included) would rather see advertisements and get tracked than pay for an internet search service.

Where are we headed with all this? No one knows. People are really bad at predicting things. I'm still waiting for flying cars. I suspect that large language models will more subtly blend into our digital lives the way Siri and Alexa and Google maps and Netflix currently do. Apple Intelligence is turning Siri into an interactive assistant that will anticipate your needs or what you're trying to accomplish, check the tone and proofread your messages, and create custom images.

How Will This Affect Education?

AI will change how students approach assignments the same way access to the internet did in the 1990s and 2000s. The bar for what is acceptable work will be raised. I suspect there will be a process that students and teachers will go through as they learn to use the technology and incorporate it into their daily workflow.

AI Adoption Lifecycle

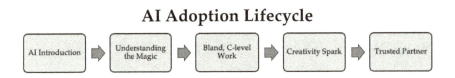

When I was first introduced to ChatGPT, I was amazed at the accuracy of the writing. I could literally have a conversation with the internet. It felt magical to type a prompt and get an

immediate response. When I presented to college faculty at the beginning of the fall semester in 2023, there were audible gasps after prompting the AI to write a grant proposal for a drone program. A process that used to take hours could be accomplished in minutes.

A closer inspection to some of the prompt responses reveals a fairly baseline, bland response. Answers seemed safe and lacked creativity. As I learned to craft more specific prompts or suggestions, it got my own creative juices flowing. I could come up with ideas and enhance them with AI. Or, if I was stuck with an idea, AI could give me suggestions to get more ideas flowing.

Currently, I use AI almost every day. AI assistants have replaced my internet searches for the most part. If I'm looking for a specific answer, I can get it instantly without having to skip past sponsored messages. While Google and other search engines do an amazing job at getting me where I want to go, if I can get there quicker and more efficiently, I will.

Teachers will probably find the lesson planning and grading helpful, but not good enough to replace good prep work. It will save time, so teachers might have more room to plan interactive activities or to customize assignments better. There will be more opportunities for reflection as to whether the activities and assignments were effective, and they will make adjustments accordingly.

Students might share a similar experience. Most of them have heard about ChatGPT or MetaAI, but the first time they use it, it will seem incredible. Some will try to submit AI-generated work on their own but will come to realize the work isn't good enough and it's easy to get caught. Eventually, AI will become a partner for the students, helping to brainstorm and organize ideas, proofreading, and acting as an interactive tutor.

Creativity

There's an idea floating around that using AI will kill creativity and all we will get are rehashed and recycled ideas the algorithm plucked from the internet. While that can be true in some cases, I mostly reject the idea. Creativity occurs when people build on the work of others. Jonas Salk couldn't have created the polio vaccine without first attending medical school to learn the existing science. Stephen King didn't invent horror fiction. Lin-Manuel Miranda never could have written the Broadway musical *Hamilton* without finding inspiration from both the Ron Chernow biography and the hip-hop music he loved. The Wright brothers wouldn't have launched the first successful manned flight without the work of Otto Lilienthal.

When I taught Macroeconomics, we discussed Paul Romer's New Growth Theory, which emphasizes that technological change is influenced by economic incentives found in markets (Romer, 1990). This means that as technological knowledge spreads around the world, people will use the existing knowledge to create new ideas that will stimulate growth. Romer was referring to economic growth, but the same idea applies to any instance where one idea inspires another, and this happens on a massive scale all the time.

If the Wright brothers stuck to selling and repairing bicycles, would we still have the airplane? Absolutely. While they were working on their airplane, the federal government-funded Samuel Langley was working on his own model. He made an unsuccessful attempt just one week before the Wright brothers' successful flight (McCullough, 2015). Albert Santos-Dumont and Gustave Whitehead were also working on heavier-than-air flying machines (Klein, 2016). The idea of human flight was in reach, and there was a world-wide race to achieve it.

Technology is the driver of simultaneous inventions (or *multiple discovery*) around the world. Most of us know that Benjamin Franklin invented the lightning rod in 1749. Most people do not know that Prokop Divis inadvertently came up with the same idea on his own five years later (information traveled a tad bit slower in the eighteenth century). Thomas Edison fought two legal battles with groups who claimed to have invented the light bulb before him. Alexander Graham Bell filed a patent for the telephone the same day as Elisha Gray (Griswold, 2013).

Apple didn't invent the technologies that went into developing the iPhone. Touchscreens already existed. Digital Cameras already existed. GPS, wireless internet, computer operating systems, web browsers and even voice-activated commands were all current technologies (Lyytinen, 2017). The creativity involved merging all those technologies and packaging the product as a "phone."

Creativity is a muscle that needs to be flexed. The more this muscle is exercised, the easier it is to generate ideas. You can't run a marathon without building up your stamina first. I've experienced this through fiction writing, songwriting, dissertation writing, and writing this book. Your creativity comes out because you're constantly asking, "How can I make this better?"

When I started writing my first novel, *Washington's Providence*, I had no idea what I was doing. I reached out to a friend, Art Edwards, who played bass in The Refreshments and later became a writer (check him out at artedwards.com). His advice was simple: get into a daily routine. I followed his advice and finished my first draft in about eight months. It reminds me of the William Faulkner quote, "I only write when I am inspired. Fortunately, I am inspired at 9 o'clock every morning" (Quote Investigator, 2013b).

Another time, I was in a songwriting group. Each week, we got a new prompt in the form of a song title and had one week to write, record, and post the song to our private Facebook group. Initially, it was stressful. How could I come up with a fully developed song and share it every seven days? The answer: schedule regular times to focus on songwriting. Some songs were keepers. Others were not, but that wasn't the point. The process of creating got much easier as the months progressed.

Students can hit their creative stride the same way. AI assistants are unparalleled in their ability to brainstorm ideas or create writing prompts. Not every idea is perfect and that's okay. A prompt for one student is going to resonate differently than it will for another. This is precisely the idea. Challenge students. Have them ask themselves, "How can I make this better?"

Potential Pitfalls

Part of the magic of ChatGPT was the amount of information it was trained on. It was indexed to the internet up to 2021. This is the version ChatGPT-3.5 users still access. ChatGPT-4, Google Gemini, Meta AI, Claude and others are continuously growing and learning through user interactions. While writing this book, I've encountered a handful of web pages that were clearly written by AI as well as AI assistant responses citing sources that were AI written.

My worry is more and more users will rely on AI to write content. This content will get posted online and AI assistants will use this content to create responses to user prompts—creating an AI feedback loop. An effort must be made by AI algorithm writers to review the data training the models. If not, biases could be magnified even further.

Final Thoughts

The idea for this book came from a presentation I prepared for k-12 teachers on using AI in the classroom. I have been to countless conferences and seminars and usually remembered 1-2 nuggets—at least for a time—and unless I put those things into practice, the nuggets disappeared. I thought I should write the kind of book I would have liked to help navigate AI—short, to-the-point, and filled with nuggets I could apply immediately.

I hope I accomplished this. I am by no means an expert. Looking at the AI Adoption Lifecycle from earlier in this chapter, I would probably place myself somewhere between the Creativity Spark and Trusted Partner. I use AI assistants almost every day. I have the Copilot and Perplexity apps on my phone and am more likely to use them to answer a question than I would a Google search.

But I don't trust all the results. If I type a prompt in the form of a question, I will get answers, but I won't accept those answers without a verifiable source. Copilot and Perplexity provide sources automatically. I mentioned earlier how Meta AI made up a song title about cheating. It makes me not want to trust anything it says, but logically I know it will get better and learn from the mistakes. There are no evil ulterior motives lurking in the background.

I also know students will use AI assistants and will be more likely to trust the information they receive. As educators, we need to prepare students with the idea that not all information they are presented with is necessarily true. Remember, they are getting a statistically likely response, not 100% verified truth. Our job as educators is to help students seek truth, whether it is pretty or not.

If you learn one lesson from this book, it is to treat AI as a tool to make your life easier. It can't replicate human connections. Think back to your favorite teachers. What made you love them? I'm sure it wasn't the engaging lesson plan where you learned the Pythagorean Theorem. It was the connection you had with a teacher where you felt genuine care. It's those connections and moments of encouragement, guidance, and understanding that leave lasting impacts. That's why we all do what we do. Use AI to help you complete the tedious tasks to leave you room for connecting with learners to ignite their potential.

Acknowledgements

No book is ready for publication the moment the author metaphorically types "the end," and this book is no different. Many people helped make this possible beyond proofreading. I've had hundreds of discussions about AI and its impact on education and appreciate all the insights and sentiments, whether I fully agree or not. None of us know it all, and all of us are partially correct. There have been too many conversations to name everyone who impacted this book.

I want to thank my wife, Molly, for putting up with my alarm going off before sunrise so I could work on the manuscript. The coffee grinder going off at 4:30am isn't the best way to start the day if you're not the one consuming the beverage. Thank you, Grace, for helping me learn eighth-grade math (again) and for letting me use your schoolwork to test prompts and come up with ideas. Special thanks to Maddie for helping design the cover with poor directions (or prompts) from me.

Thank you to Ken Gunter for going through the first version of the manuscript and for alleviating my insecurities about whether the book will be helpful to anyone by saying, "If an old, retired teacher can read this and understand how AI will help in the classroom, it should benefit everyone."

I am extremely grateful to the teachers and administrators who read early drafts and provided feedback. Kimberly Brown and Dr. Jill Schreiber, thank you for the kind words and great suggestions. To Dr. Matt Cardin, thank you for pointing out ways to make the blurb on the back cover more effective.

I can't begin to quantify how appreciative I am with the help provided by (soon to be doctor) Jennifer Bertolet. Her line-by-line examination saved me time and embarrassment, and the manuscript is better because of her help.

Finally, I need to thank *you*, dear reader. I suspect a lot of the material covered will be obsolete in the near future, but I hope it's because we've all adapted, and our profession has embraced the technology. I hope my small contribution helps move the needle.

Although the book is about using AI, I wrote every word not attributed to one of the AI assistants. Any inaccuracies are on me. When deciding whether to write this book, I found a number of publications that were clearly written by AI. This one is not.

Please spread the word. Share this with your colleagues. (Better yet, buy a copy for everyone in your school!) Leave an honest review or connect with me on LinkedIn. We can even schedule a video conference with your school. I'd love to know what worked for you and what needs more development. We're all on this learning journey together.

References

Altchek, A. (2024). SATs are back. Dartmouth is the first Ivy League to reverse course after pledging to remove standardized test requirement. Business Insider.

Berkin, C., Miller, C., Cherny, R., & Gormly, J. (2015). Making American A history of the United States (7th ed.). Cengage Learning.

Bianchi, F., Kalluri, P., Durmus, E., Ladhak, F., Cheng, M., Nozza, D., Hashimoto, T., Jurafsky, D., Zou, J., & Caliskan, A. (2023). Easily Accessible Text-to-Image Generation Amplifies Demographic Stereotypes at Large Scale. Proceedings of the 2023 ACM Conference on Fairness, Accountability, and Transparency, 1493–1504. https://doi.org/10.1145/3593013.3594095

Bowen, J. A., & Watson, C. E. (2024). Teaching with AI: A practical guide to a new era of human learning. Johns Hopkins University Press.

Brinkman, B. (2012). An Analysis of Student Privacy Rights in the Use of Plagiarism Detection Systems. Science and Engineering Ethics, 19, 1255 - 1266.

Cain, A. (2017, September 15). The life and death of Microsoft clippy, the paper clip the world loved to hate. Artsy. https://www.artsy.net/article/artsy-editorial-life-death-microsoft-clippy-paper-clip-loved-hate

Cagle, R. (2024, May 13). Arizona schools can't ignore AI. this is

how they use it responsibly. The Arizona Republic.
https://www.azcentral.com/story/opinion/op-
ed/2024/05/13/ai-change-school-teaching-work-use-
responsibly/73646855007/

Chase, C. (2023, November 4). Exploring Forms of Feedback
with AI. IT Teaching Resources.
https://teachingresources.stanford.edu/resources/feedbac
k-from-generative-ai/

Chechitelli, A. (2023, May 23). AI writing detection update
from Turnitin's chief product officer. Canada (English).
https://www.turnitin.com/blog/ai-writing-detection-
update-from-turnitins-chief-product-officer

Cooper, K. (2023, October 6). OpenAI GPT-3: Everything you
need to know [updated]. Springboard Blog.
https://www.springboard.com/blog/data-
science/machine-learning-gpt-3-open-ai/

Crowley, M. (2024, July 24). Meta launches biggest AI model
ever. Meta launches biggest AI model ever | AI Tool
Report. https://www.aitoolreport.com/articles/meta-
launches-biggest-ai-model-
ever?utm_source=aitoolreport.beehiiv.com&utm_medium=
newsletter&utm_campaign=meta-launches-biggest-ai-
model-ever

Duarte, F. (2024, June 8). Number of CHATGPT users (Jun
2024). Exploding Topics.
https://explodingtopics.com/blog/chatgpt-users

Dubner, S. J. (2024, February 21). Is Google getting worse?

(update). Freakonomics.
https://freakonomics.com/podcast/is-google-getting-worse-update/

Downey, C. J., Steffy, B. E., Poston, W. K., & English, F. W. (2009). Introduction. In 50 Ways to Close the Achievement Gap (3 ed., pp. 1-8). Corwin Press, https://doi.org/10.4135/9781452218915

Dweck, C. S. (2006). Mindset: The New Psychology of Success. Ballantine Books.

Gilbert, D. (2024, February 22). Google's "woke" image generator shows the limitations of ai. Wired. https://www.wired.com/story/google-gemini-woke-ai-image-generation/

Grammarly. (2024). Features. https://www.grammarly.com/features

Google. (n.d.). What is cloud computing? Google. https://cloud.google.com/learn/what-is-cloud-computing

Gordon, R. (2022, October 27). 3 questions: How AI image generators work. 3 Questions: How AI image generators work | MIT CSAIL. https://www.csail.mit.edu/news/3-questions-how-ai-image-generators-work

Griffin, Kevin. (2004). *Better Than Ezra Live at the House of Blues*. Sanctuary Records [DVD].

Griswold, M. (2013, May 17). Multiple simultaneous invention. The Long Nose.

https://thelongnose.com/blog/2013/4/29/multiple-simultaneous-invention

Harris, A., & Jones, M. (2020). Leading for equity. In System Recall: Leading for Equity and Excellence in Education (pp. 63-76). Corwin, https://doi.org/10.4135/9781071873113

Jimenez, K. (2023, February 2). "This shouldn't be a surprise" The education community shares mixed reactions to ChatGPT. USA Today. https://www.usatoday.com/story/news/education/2023/01/30/chatgpt-going-banned-teachers-sound-alarm-new-ai-tech/11069593002/

Johnson, A. (2017). Six lesson plan formats. https://cornerstone.lib.mnsu.edu/eec-fac-pubs/1136

Johnsen, S. K. (2023b). Learning environments. Gifted Child Today, 46(4), 233–234. https://doi.org/10.1177/10762175231186678

Khan, S. (2024). Brave new words: How AI will revolutionize education (and why that's a good thing). New York: Viking.

Kim, C., & Araujo, J. (2021, October 12). Automated Grading Systems. OxJournal. https://www.oxjournal.org/automated-grading/

Klein, C. (2016, August 14). Who was first in Flight?. History.com. https://www.history.com/news/history-faceoff-who-was-first-in-flight

Kuntz, D. (2024, May 8). Um teaching graduate jumps aboard

AI Education Train. University of Montana.
https://www.umt.edu/news/2024/05/050824simo.php

Lakhani, K. (2023, August 4). AI won't replace humans - but humans with AI will replace humans without AI. Harvard Business Review. https://hbr.org/2023/08/ai-wont-replace-humans-but-humans-with-ai-will-replace-humans-without-ai

Liles, J. (2023, January 31). CHATGPT declines request for poem admiring Trump, but Biden query is successful. Snopes. https://www.snopes.com/fact-check/chatgpt-trump-admiring-poem/

Lyytinen, K. (2017, June 29). Understanding the real innovation behind the iPhone. Scientific American. https://www.scientificamerican.com/article/understanding-the-real-innovation-behind-the-iphone/

Manning, A. J. (2024, May 8). How is generative AI changing education?. Harvard Gazette. https://news.harvard.edu/gazette/story/2024/05/how-is-generative-ai-changing-education-artificial-intelligence/

Mason, J., & Renshaw, J. (2023b, June 26). US to spend $42 billion to make internet access universal by 2030. United States. https://www.reuters.com/world/us/biden-detail-plans-42-billion-investment-us-internet-access-2023-06-26/

McCabe, D. L., Treviño, L. K., & Butterfield, K. D. (2012). Cheating in college why students do it and what educators can do about it. Johns Hopkins University Press.

McCracken, H. (2024, April 24). Meta AI is a serious CHATGPT rival. but it could be so much ... Plugged In. https://www.fastcompany.com/91110823/meta-ai-facebook-instagram-whatsapp-messenger

McCullough, D. G. (2015). The Wright brothers (First Simon & Schuster hardcover edition.). Simon & Schuster.

Motoki, F., Pinho Neto, V., & Rodrigues, V. (2024). More human than human: measuring ChatGPT political bias. Public Choice, 198(1–2), 3–23. https://doi.org/10.1007/s11127-023-01097-2

Neumeister, L. (2023, June 22). Lawyers submitted bogus case law created by CHATGPT. A judge fined them $5,000. AP News. https://apnews.com/article/artificial-intelligence-chatgpt-fake-case-lawyers-d6ae9fa79d0542db9e1455397aef381c

Ng, A. (2023, October). AI isn't the problem - it's the solution. Andrew Ng: AI isn't the problem - it's the solution | TED Talk. https://www.ted.com/talks/andrew_ng_ai_isn_t_the_problem_it_s_the_solution/transcript

O'Neil, C. (2017, April). The era of blind faith in big data must end. Cathy O'Neil: The era of blind faith in big data must end | TED Talk. https://www.ted.com/talks/cathy_o_neil_the_era_of_blind_faith_in_big_data_must_end?delay=0s&subtitle=en

OpenAi. (n.d.). Is CHATGPT biased? | openai help center. Educator FAQ.

https://help.openai.com/en/articles/8313359-is-chatgpt-biased

Palmer, E. (2023, December 14). Michael Cohen lawyer's citing of fictional case raises CHATGPT suspicions. Newsweek. https://www.newsweek.com/michael-cohen-lawyer-chatgpt-court-cases-ai-1852530

Quote Investigator. (2013a, October 20). Quote origin: It's difficult to make predictions, especially about the future. https://quoteinvestigator.com/2013/10/20/no-predict/

Quote Investigator. (2013b, October 30). Quote origin: I only write when inspiration strikes. Fortunately it strikes at nine every morning. https://quoteinvestigator.com/2013/10/30/inspire-nine/

Ré, C. (2023, April 20). Understanding the ingredients in CHATGPT is simpler than you think. Hazy Research. https://hazyresearch.stanford.edu/blog/2023-04-20-how-chatgpt-works

Romer, P. M. (1990). Endogenous Technological Change. The Journal of Political Economy, 98(5), S71–S102. https://doi.org/10.1086/261725

Ryan, E. (2023, September 11). Ethical Implications of ChatGPT. Scribbr. https://www.scribbr.com/ai-tools/chatgpt-ethics/

Serdyukov, P., & Ryan, M. (2008a). Writing effective lesson plans: The 5-star approach. Pearson Allyn and Bacon.

Shute, V. J. (2008). Focus on Formative Feedback. Review of

Educational Research, 78(1), 153–189.
https://doi.org/10.3102/0034654307313795

Terry, O. K. (2023, May 17). Opinion: I'm a student. you have no idea how much we're using CHATGPT. The Chronicle of Higher Education. https://www.chronicle.com/article/im-a-student-you-have-no-idea-how-much-were-using-chatgpt

theaimastery.com. (2023). Mastering the Art of Prompt Engineering. Common Mistakes You Need To Avoid When Crafting ChatGPT Prompts. https://portal.theaimastery.com/

The Ohio State University. (n.d.). AI teaching strategies: Having conversations with students. Teaching and Learning Resource Center. https://teaching.resources.osu.edu/teaching-topics/ai-teaching-strategies-having

Thomson, T. J., & Thomas, R. (2023, July 9). Ageism, sexism, classism and more: 7 examples of bias in AI-generated images. The Conversation. https://theconversation.com/ageism-sexism-classism-and-more-7-examples-of-bias-in-ai-generated-images-208748#:~:text=There%20were%20also%20notable%20differences,of%20more%20fluid%20gender%20expression.

Tray.io. (2019a, August 29). How do apis work? an in-depth guide. https://tray.io/blog/how-do-apis-work

Tyson, N.D. (2013, April 14). When Students cheat on exams it's because our School System values grades more than Students value learning. [Post]. X.

https://x.com/neiltyson/status/323495818889949184

Waltzer, T., & Dahl, A. (2023). Why do students cheat? Perceptions, evaluations, and motivations. Ethics & Behavior, 33(2), 130–150. https://doi.org/10.1080/10508422.2022.2026775

Wikimedia Foundation. (2024, May 15). Size of wikipedia. Wikipedia. https://en.wikipedia.org/wiki/Wikipedia:Size_of_Wikipedia

Chris LaFata is the Dean of Arts, Sciences, Business, & IT at North Arkansas College. Prior to that, he spent over 20 years teaching college economics at a variety of colleges and universities. He is the author of the novel, Washington's Providence. In his spare time, he can be found cheering on his daughters' volleyball teams, recording music, or catching up on sleep.

You can connect with him on LinkedIn: https://www.linkedin.com/in/chrislafata/